Porsche
Boxster Story

Other titles by the Paul Frère

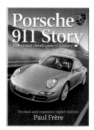

PORSCHE 911 STORY
The entire development history
Eighth edition
Paul Frère
ISBN 1 84425 301 5
£25.00

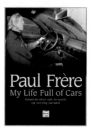

MY LIFE FULL OF CARS
Behind the wheel with the
world's top motoring journalist
Paul Frère
ISBN 1 85960 670 9
£19.99

Porsche
Boxster Story
The entire development history

Paul Frère

First published in June 2006

A catalogue record for this book is available from the British Library

ISBN 1 84425 009 1

Library of Congress catalog card no 2005925517

Published by Haynes Publishing, Sparkford, Yeovil, Somerset BA22 7JJ, UK
Tel: 01963 442030 Fax: 01963 440001
Int. tel: +44 1963 442030
Int. fax: +44 1963 440001
E-mail: sales@haynes.co.uk
Website: www.haynes.co.uk

Haynes North America Inc, 861 Lawrence Drive, Newbury Park, California 91320, USA.

Designed by Richard Parsons

Printed and bound in Britain by
J. H. Haynes & Co. Ltd, Sparkford

Photographic Credits
All photographs and illustrations were provided by Dr Ing. h. c. F. Porsche AG with the following exceptions:

John Colley 20/21, 22/23, 36, 44/45, 54/55, 57, 64/65, 80, 81 82/83, 110/111

LAT Photographic 63, 74/75, 76, 77, 78/79

Peter Robain 139/137, 143, 156, 161, 166, 172/173, 175 top, 180

Authors Acknowledgements
My warmest thanks go to Porsche's Development chief Dipl-Ing Wolfgang Dürheimer and his staff and to Public Relations manager Anton Hunger and his crew, who were immensely helpful in providing me with technical information without which this book could never have been written.

Contents

Why the Boxster?

Up until 1990, Porsche had been a profitable company. It could look back on forty years of almost unprecedented success in motor sport, including twelve victories (with four more to follow) in the celebrated Le Mans 24-hours race. Not only that, but three Formula 1 World Championships for Porsche engines had further boosted the company's image, while the 911 had become a legend among sports cars.

Look closer, however, and only the Porsche 356, which had started life as a sporting derivative of the VW Beetle, and the 911 itself had been successful over an extended period. Even if the late-series 928, the 944 Turbo and 944 S2 – and the final 968 – were excellent cars in their own right, these front-engined models were ultimately a marketing misjudgement. Intended as a successor to the 911, the V8-engined 928 was too bulky and not agile enough with early models not fast enough, while a four-cylinder engine, however good, was not deemed prestigious enough for sports cars in the price class to which the 944 and 968 belonged. The cars were also high-priced, due in part to not sharing components with other Porsche models.

A further reason for Porsche stumbling was that in the 1980s the 911 in particular had sold strongly in the United States

and sales of all models had boomed in a newly buoyant Britain. This had made the management complacent and little was done to modernise production facilities and reduce manufacturing costs. In 1991, with the world economy slipping into depression, for the first time Porsche suffered serious losses.

This is when Dr Wendelin Wiedeking, a production expert who had been with Porsche in earlier times, was chosen as Managing Director by the Supervising Board. He, in turn, chose as engineering director, responsible for car development, Horst Marchart, a brilliant engineer who had been with Porsche in various positions from the beginning of his career.

The pragmatic Wiedeking did not hesitate to send a group of engineers to Japan to gather information about the latest Japanese production techniques. By that time the development potential of the original air-cooled 911 was nearing its end, and a complete redesign would soon be needed to meet ever-stricter exhaust emission, passive safety and noise requirements. Fortunately, the last evolution of the original 911,

▼ This concept model first exhibited at Detroit in 1993 heralded the arrival of the Boxster in 1996

▲ Whichever way
you looked at it, the
1993 Boxster concept
car was stylish,
and exactly what
enthusiasts expected
from Porsche

the 993-series, was already in the pipeline and was to be a great success, leaving enough time for a completely new range of models to be developed.

Wiedeking's marketing plan was to develop two new models. One – coded the 996 – would continue the 911 line, and the other, possibly inspired by the enormous success of the Mazda MX-5 (or Miata), would be a mid-engined open two-seater to be sold at a lower price as an 'entry-level' Porsche. The secret was that both models would share as many components as possible.

Following the decision to make a roadster, styling chief Harm Lagaay and his crew sat down to produce various styling studies for the new car. However, the most promising design turned out to be for a concept model destined for the Detroit Auto Show. This concept was the Boxster, the name being a contraction of the words Boxer (German for a horizontally-opposed engine) and Roadster.

Inspired by the first ever Porsche, chassis number 356–001, and by the famous 550 racing Spyders of the 1950s, both these being mid-engined, the hurriedly-built Boxster concept was a

star of the Detroit Auto Show of 1993. It was quite small, looked exciting, and was exactly what enthusiasts expected from Porsche. It raised high expectations.

So close, but 40 years apart: 550 Spyder (above) and 986 Boxster (left)

As the Boxster (internally known as 986) and the new 911 were to share the largest possible number of components, it was clear that the two teams responsible for their development would have to work closely together. To accelerate development further, for the first time all the major external suppliers were instructed about Porsche's plans as soon as the broad lines of the project had been laid down and were involved from the outset in the development of the new models.

This is what Porsche calls 'Simultaneous Engineering', and was possible because the cars were designed to be assembled from bought-in modules, pre-assembled and tested by the suppliers: for example such important units as the front and rear suspensions, complete with steering gear; the transmission; and the dashboard assembly with instruments, air conditioning, steering column, wiring and pedals.

Apart from minor variations to accommodate their different weight distribution, the higher power of the 996-series 911's

▲ Except for the
front skirt the Boxster
shared the entire front
part of the body with
the 996-series 911

engine, and the costlier car's more luxurious equipment, the two models shared their entire front structure, including the dashboard assembly, the front suspension and the steering, and also most components of the flat-six engine and of the transmission. The engines differ only in their cubic capacity. Furthermore, as the rule was that when a choice had to be made between two possible solutions, priority was to be given to the 996, there were probably some instances in which the Boxster benefited from the more sophisticated solutions demanded for the more expensive model.

It has to be said, however, that where the parts sharing was obvious, this was not well accepted by 996-series 911 clientele who had paid a lot more for a car which was difficult to differentiate from a cheaper Boxster when it appeared in the

▼ **Ghosted view of the 1997 model Porsche Boxster**

▲ Horst Marchart,
Porsche's Chief
of Development
from 1992 to his
retirement in 2001.
The 986 Boxster
and 996 Carrera
were developed
under his leadership

◤ Dr Wolfgang
Dürheimer
succeeded Horst
Marchart as
Porsche's Chief
of Development

▶ Dr Wendelin
Wiedeking, Porsche's
Managing Director
since 1991

rear-view mirror of other road users. For this reason, when the time came for a minor facelift of the 996, Porsche conceded the point and gave the more expensive model differently-shaped lighting units.

For similar marketing reasons Porsche was determined that the 996 and its successors in the 911 model line would always provide a marginally higher performance than the fastest Boxster – thereby offering tuning specialists the chance to turn their attention to tweaking the Boxster. Following this logic, as the power and performance of the 911 models have progressively increased, the Boxster has kept pace, while always remaining a step below its bigger brother: first came a capacity increase from 2.5 litres to 2.7 litres, then the addition of the Boxster S powered by a 3.2-litre engine.

Having been developed in parallel, the Boxster and the 996-series 911 were ready for production simultaneously. As by that time the 993-series 911 was still selling strongly, only commercial considerations prompted Porsche to introduce the Boxster one year before the 996-series 911.

Major development targets specific to the Boxster were:

- Mid-engine technology
- Typical Porsche styling
- Excellent ergonomics for both driver and passenger
- Good looks, despite increasingly severe environmental requirements
- Water cooling, to meet worldwide emission and noise regulations while retaining good fuel economy and high specific power
- Compatibility with existing mass-produced components, such as air conditioning systems
- Minimization of logistic costs
- Ease of production and low production times while retaining highest quality
- Production compatible with pre-assembled modules, such as the dash structure and the soft top and its mechanism.

When the production Boxster was unveiled at the Paris Salon in September 1996, it was a larger car than the concept model of 1993. This was due not only to sharing a large number of components with the 996-series 911, but mainly because the production Boxster had to meet worldwide safety and emission requirements, and had to provide weather protection and adequate comfort and luggage space. The general shape still vividly recalled the famous racing Spyders, but, apart from the size, many details were different from those on the original concept car. One was that the air intakes for the engine compartment had been moved from their original position on the sills, ahead of the rear wheels, to a position high up in the body sides. This was because in the lower position they would have drawn in too much dust and dirt. Also, the front overhang was longer – more so than the stylists would have liked – as a result of crash-test and luggage-stowage requirements.

Nevertheless, the car was an immediate success and when one year later the 996-series 911 replaced the 993-series, the assembly line in the Stuttgart-Zuffenhausen factory soon became insufficient to meet demand. Boxster assembly was therefore additionally entrusted to the Valmet company

▶ The first official picture of the Boxster in March 1996

in Finland, the cars being built to the same quality standards as those constructed in Zuffenhausen. This cooperation has raised Porsche's production to a fairly steady 50,000 cars annually, roughly equally split between the Boxster and 911 ranges.

When Porsche decided to develop the Boxster, 25 years had elapsed since the company had designed an open – or semi-open – car from scratch. Any experience gained from the development of the Targa-top 914 had been rendered useless by today's much higher passive safety requirements.

When designing an open car, the two biggest challenges to be met are to achieve adequate torsional and beam stiffness and good crash safety, especially in the case of roll-over, in both cases without unduly increasing the car's weight. The roll-over problem is easily understandable, and can be met by extremely stiff windscreen pillars and roll-over bars behind the seats. Torsional and beam stiffness are important to avoid rattles and scuttle-shake, but torsional stiffness is also very important for predictable

handling, as understeer and oversteer depend to a large extent on the interaction of the front and rear suspensions and this in turn depends upon the degree of roll stiffness provided by the body structure itself. Side intrusion is also a bigger problem in an open car than in a closed one because there is no roof structure to brace the door apertures.

Further to this, the crash behaviour of a mid-engined car is different from that of more conventional cars, especially in frontal crashes. On one hand the absence of an engine ahead of the driver and passenger allows more space for energy absorption by deformation of the frontal structure. On the other hand, however, the kinetic energy of the entire power unit as it tries to break loose in an accident must be absorbed by the deformation of the structure behind the cockpit. The engine mountings must also be strong enough to prevent the engine from penetrating the passenger compartment.

In a roadster, all these rigidity and safety requirements must be compatible with the installation of the mechanical units, the need for luggage space, the achievement of satisfactory aerodynamic efficiency, and the evolution of eye-catching styling incorporating a harmonious design of soft top. The last challenge is particularly real, as space for the soft top is always going to be limited because it has to be located just above the engine. All these requirements easily explain why the Boxster is a larger car than both the 550 Spyder and the original concept car. To have

The front and rear
boots each had a
capacity of 130 litres

achieved an overall kerb weight of only 1,250kg is thus highly
commendable, considering the excellent rigidity of the roofless
body and the lavish specification, which includes a power-
operated soft top.

In 1993, when the decision was taken to develop two
completely new models sharing a large number of components,
Porsche had a suitable engine almost ready: a water-cooled
racing engine which, having been developed from the production
911 engine, could, to a large extent, have been produced on the
existing facilities. In fact this is what Porsche did in the case of its
highest-performance models, the 996-series 911 GT3, the Turbo
and the G12. But for the new bigger-volume range Porsche
wanted a more refined and lighter engine more compatible with
the latest production systems.

PART 1

Introducing the Boxster

CHAPTER 1

The body structure

As with the 996-series 911, the entire Boxster body structure and all its panels are made of steel. Everything is zinc-coated on both sides – the only exception being the high-resistance boron alloy-steel components, which are inherently rustproof. Much weight has been saved on the body structure by the widespread use of modern assembly techniques such as laser welding and the use of high-resistance steel components such as bake-hardened steel sheets, tailored blanks (sheet metal of different gauges and characteristics, laser-welded before forming) and boron alloy steel. Porsche gives a ten-year warranty against rust perforation of all bodyshell components, without requiring any specific anti-rust treatment over this period.

The body structure, combining maximum rigidity with light weight, was developed on computers. Standard practice today, this saves much time and money, because most of the crash tests can be computer-simulated, making it possible to optimise the structure before any real tests are carried out. An important contribution to torsional stiffness is made by the diagonal bracing of both ends of the bodyshell; at the rear this also contributes to the firm location of the suspension subframe. The static torsional stiffness of the Boxster is 11,000 Nm/degree with the hood open,

▶ In a front-end collision, the impact is absorbed first by the bumper bar behind the front skirt and then by deformable crash boxes, which are in turn bolted to the lower longitudinal members of the main body structure. The comparatively inexpensive crash boxes are designed to absorb energy in low-speed collisions, protecting the main body structure, and must be replaced when the damage is repaired. Rear-end crash protection is, in principle, similar to front-end protection

▶ General view of the Boxster's body structure

11,500Nm/degree with the hood closed and 12,500Nm/degree with the hardtop in place. These figures exceed by 55 per cent those of the 993-series 911 Cabriolet. Not surprisingly, however, they are still way behind those of the 996-series 911 coupé, which is nearly three times as torsionally stiff as the open Boxster – the structural roof making all the difference. But the Boxster is easily stiff enough to prevent scuttle-shake and other problems, as well as to ensure top class handling.

The Boxster's final shape was designed by American-born Grant Larson under the leadership of chief stylist Harm Lagaay, who was also responsible for the 996-series 911 coupé. Lagaay's brief also included coordination of the parallel 986 and 996 projects and cooperation with the aerodynamicists and engineers responsible for the structural part of the body.

In accordance with Porsche's common parts and components policy, the Boxster and the 996-series 911 share the entire front part of the body, internal and external pressings, up to and including the doors. A very commendable achievement is the drag coefficient of only 0.31 with the soft top in place, a figure difficult to obtain with such a short superstructure and one achieved by attention to detail in Porsche's own wind tunnel in Weissach.

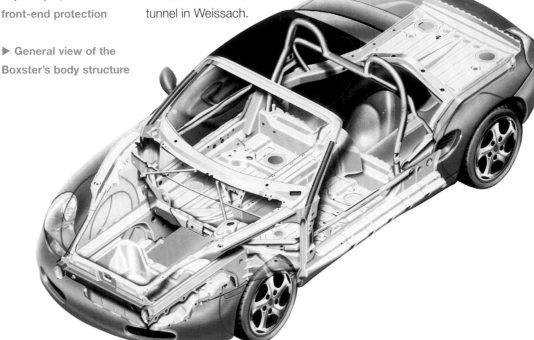

The wheelbase of the Boxster is 65mm longer than that of the 996-series 911, but the car's overall length is 120mm shorter, thanks to a shorter rear overhang, while width and height are identical to those of the 911. Its kerb weight (ready to be driven, with a full tank and all other liquids) is 1,250kg, of which the front axle carries 47 per cent and the rear axle 53 per cent. This distribution hardly varies with driver and passenger on board, the seat position being fairly close to the centre of gravity; only the level of the fuel in the 60-litre tank located just behind the front wheel axis affects the weight distribution.

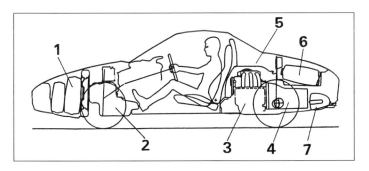

◀ General layout of the
Porsche Boxster

1 Front boot
2 Fuel tank
3 Engine
4 Gearbox
5 Hood recess
6 Rear boot
7 Tail exhaust silencer

Front views of the
early 996-series
911 (above) and
the Boxster (right)
compared

PASSIVE SAFETY

In a frontal crash, the impact forces first affect the plastic-clad
aluminium bumper. This is carried by a pair of tubes bolted to
the structural longitudinal members. These tubes, which are
easily replaceable, are designed to deform and absorb energy
before the rest of the body structure is involved, avoiding
expensive repairs in the case of sub-8mph impacts. The same
protection system is also used at the rear of the car. In a
more severe accident the forces are then channelled into the
floorpan's longitudinal members, into the centre tunnel and
into the suspension turrets. The underfloor fuel tank lies
behind the deformable zone and is protected by the front
suspension crossmember.

Side intrusions are taken care of by the very robust floorpan
and body sides, the high-resistance boron alloy steel profiles
inside the doors, the welded-in seat platform, which also
contributes to the structural stiffness of the floorpan, and the
very rigid B-pillar assembly. In addition the locks firmly retain the
doors, which actually stretch under impact.

To protect the firmly belted-up driver and passenger in a roll-over, the windscreen pillars are reinforced by a strong boron alloy steel tube welded to the front door pillars and by two roll-over hoops behind the seats, closely following the shape of the seat backs and with integrated headrests. The three-piece steering column has a deformable harmonica-like tube that prevents penetration of the column into the cabin in a frontal crash. In addition, driver and passenger are protected by two full-size airbags. A sensor is incorporated in each seat cushion and recognises whether the passenger seat is occupied, thus avoiding the unnecessary deployment of an airbag in the event of an accident. The crash-sensor module, on the left-hand panel of the central tunnel, not only triggers the airbags but also records the deceleration process, which can be analysed after an accident.

EXTERNAL EQUIPMENT

The electrically-operated folding hood comes without internal lining and has a flexible PVC rear window. When folded it disappears into a special recess, thanks to a novel folding

technique, and is partially covered by an automatically-operated metal cover. In most roadsters the forward part of the folding hood folds back some 180° before the rest folds down into the open position. In the Boxster the hood folds to form a 'Z' when viewed from the side, in such a way that it folds with the external surface up. This results in a very flat package which fits into a shallow hood box above the engine compartment. When folded, only a part of the hood remains visible, flush with the hinged hood cover, which opens and closes automatically when the hood is operated. The operating mechanism is secured to the side panels of the hood box and is actuated from the remote electric motor by flexible shafts. The hood frame is mostly made up of die-cast magnesium parts and weighs only 12.8kg.

The electrically-operated soft top can be opened or closed in just 12 seconds

For reasons of cost and weight, the anchorage of the hood to the windscreen frame is by hand, but only requires operating a single central handle on the hood header-rail. The rest is entirely automatic, via a switch on the central tunnel; first, though, the handbrake has to be applied and the ignition has to be in the 'on' position. If the side windows are closed, they drop 6mm to disengage from the hood frame's rubber seals as soon as a door handle – interior or exterior – is moved. The entire opening or closing process takes only 12 seconds.

The hood is designed so that when raised there is the minimum possible wind noise. In the open position, meanwhile, turbulence over the cockpit can be drastically reduced by the optional wind deflector. This consists of two triangular

wire-mesh inserts that fit into the two roll-over hoops and
one small scratch-proof transparent panel, which is a slide-
fit between them. These form a barrier against the flow of air
which, at speed, turns back to fill the low-pressure zone in the
cockpit. The deflector can remain in place when the hood is up.

In contrast to earlier Porsches the fuel filler cap is in the
right-hand front wing and its cover is locked by the central
locking system. As with the 993-series 911, the headlight
assemblies are instantly removable by turning a lever inside
the luggage compartment; they incorporate a halogen H7
headlamp, a fog light, a parking light and the indicator. A
manual beam adjustment is provided. The external glass
is shock-resistant and covered by a transparent scratch-
resistant lacquer.

Several panels protect and smooth the underbody,
optimising the Boxster's aerodynamic efficiency. The panels
are made of recycled plastic and are easily removable for
access to the mechanicals. The body structure is further
shielded from dirt and corrosion by plastic wheelarch inserts.

AERODYNAMIC EFFICIENCY

It is not easy to achieve a low drag coefficient in a roadster, even in its closed configuration, but meticulous detail work has resulted in a drag coefficient (C_d) of 0.31, the same as for the 996-series 911 coupé, together with impressive figures for front and rear lift. A clever aerodynamic detail is the ducting of the air cooling the two front-mounted radiators. The air enters through openings in the front skirt and exits vertically just ahead of the front wheels, thereby reducing their aerodynamic resistance and almost compensating for the drag caused by the radiators.

The electrically-operated retractable rear spoiler comes up at a speed of 75mph and is retracted as the speed drops below 50mph. This accounts for a drag reduction of 4 per cent and for a reduction in rear lift of 31 per cent. The plastic underbody panels mentioned above contribute a further 10 per cent reduction in drag and shave rear lift by no less than 33 per cent.

For those interested in the finer detail, at the car's maximum speed of 149mph the total lift force acting on the car is 59kg, of which 32kg acts on the front axle and 27kg on the rear axle. These figures are not as good as for the 996-series 911 coupé,

▼ The rear spoiler raises automatically when speed reaches 75mph and retracts when speed drops below 50mph

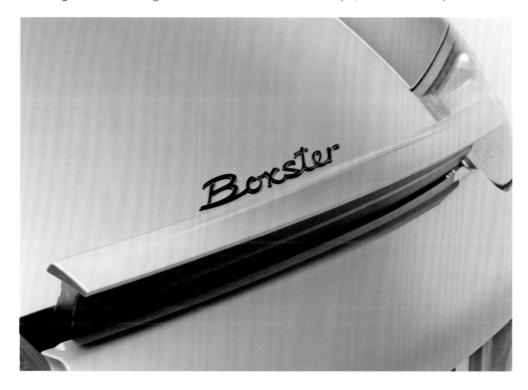

but the main point is that lift on the rear axle is lower than that over the front axle. This means that as speed is increased, so the grip of the front wheels decreases faster than the grip of the rear wheels and consequently the car's tendency to understeer increases – as is desirable for stability in high-speed cornering.

INTERIOR EQUIPMENT

The plastics used in the interior have been chosen for their recyclability, for their absence of smell, and for the lack of gaseous emissions which in time can form deposits on the windows. Most of the large plastic components, such as the instrument panel and the door casings, are part of the recyclable propylene family. The base is polypropylene, a fairly rigid material, and is covered by a softer plastic which can optionally be replaced with leather. The complex module carrying the instrument cluster, the passenger airbag, the central control unit with its large air outlet, all the switchgear, the climate-control, the radio and the optional navigation system is completely pre-assembled before a robot inserts it in the car. A large choice of

radios, CD players, telephones and sat-nav systems has always been offered, the options changing over successive model years.

The seats were newly designed by Porsche for the Boxster and 911, and have an integral headrest on a new lightweight frame. The central surface of the seat and backrest are cloth and the surrounds are artificial PVC-free leather; full leather seats are an option. The longitudinal and height adjustments are manual, while rake is adjusted electrically. Full electrical adjustment is an option. The backrest can be released and folded forward from either side and retains its original position when raised again. The back of the squab carries a large pocket and a clothes hook. A glovebox is provided at the rear of the centre console, which carries the switches for the windows and the hood – which can also be operated from the ignition key by remote control.

Only three dials are provided in the instrument cluster. The rev-counter, true to Porsche tradition, is directly in front of the driver and is the largest dial; it is flanked on the left by the speedometer and on the right by the fuel and water-temperature gauges. In the speedometer are a digital mileometer and trip recorder and, if fitted, a Tempomat (speed control) warning light; in the rev-counter is a digital speedometer showing miles or kilometres at the push of a button and the (optional) on-board computer display, while the right-hand dial houses a digital clock and an oil-level gauge, as well as, if applicable, the LED display for the Tiptronic transmission.

To save weight both the accelerator pedal and the hollow clutch pedal are in plastic, while the brake pedal is in aluminium; in contrast to former Porsche practice, the pedals are of the pendant type.

On the driver's side, two levers in the sill open the front and rear boots via cables. The 130-litre front boot gives access to the emergency spare wheel mounted vertically against the rear wall of the boot and hiding the tools and jack, and to the battery, centrally located just ahead of the windscreen. The water tank for the screen washers and – if fitted – the headlamp washers is also in the front boot, as is the brake fluid reservoir. The rear boot, also of 130-litre capacity, houses the engine-oil dipstick and the oil and coolant fillers.

▼ The oil dipstick, oil filler and coolant filler are accessed from the rear boot. All other engine servicing is performed from underneath the car

Access to the engine is by removing a cover at the bottom of the hood container and another in the firewall between engine and cockpit. Except for checking and topping-up the levels, all normal engine servicing is carried out from underneath the car.

COCKPIT HEATING AND AIR CONDITIONING

Although air conditioning was an option for the basic Boxster, many cars were delivered with full automatic air conditioning, and so this is what is described here. In cars fitted only with a heating and ventilating system, the installation is identical, with the omission of the cooling equipment, namely the compressor, and the condensers located in the front wheel housings, ahead of the engine coolant radiators, and the vaporiser inside the dash mounted air distributor unit.

With or without air conditioning, a single air distributor unit, located within the dash structure, contains the entire system, heating or cooling (with air conditioning only) the fresh or recirculated air and distributing it at the required temperature to the various outlets inside the cockpit. The system comprises the engine coolant/air heat exchanger of the heating system,

the vaporiser in which the incoming air is cooled (air conditioning only), the intake and outlet air temperature sensors, the four-speed fan and the motor operating the flaps to obtain the required mixture of fresh, warmed or (in case of air conditioning) cooled air to achieve the correct air temperature. Two further sensors register the cockpit air temperature and the temperature under sun exposure. To minimise the power absorbed by the air compressor, its output is always limited to the minimum required, and it is disconnected automatically if the outside temperature falls below +2°C or when the air conditioning is switched off manually. It is also switched off to avoid power absorption when starting the engine and for the following seven seconds, as well as for 15 seconds whenever the engine is operated at full load.

ANTI-THEFT SYSTEMS

Two levels of anti-theft equipment are available. The standard equipment comprises only the car's individual ignition key, which incorporates a battery and a radio transponder. As well as operating the ignition, the starter and the steering column lock in the normal way, and the central-locking system by remote control, as an essential anti-theft measure, the engine management DME (Digital Motor Electronics) unit is not energised unless the doors have been unlocked by remote control.

In the optional equipment, the remote control additionally energises an alarm system operating a horn and an infrared sensor reacting to any movement inside the car. A button on the key unlocks the rear boot and the tank filler if required.

▲ The body of the Boxster remained externally unchanged from the start of production to 2002

◀ Routine engine servicing is carried out from beneath the car. Removing the cover at the bottom of the hood container gives access to the top of the engine for other tasks, including cleaning!

CHAPTER 2

Engine and transmission

THE 2.5-LITRE M96/20 ENGINE

The M96/20 engine of the Boxster and the M96/01 engine of the 996-series 911, both liquid-cooled, were designed and developed from scratch and share most of their components, except those related to their cubic capacities. With a bore of 85.5mm and a stroke of 72mm, the M96/20 engine has a displacement of 2,480cc. It develops 201bhp (204PS) at 6,000rpm with a rev limit of 6,700rpm and maximum torque of 180lb ft (244Nm) at 4,500rpm.

The only item of the earlier Porsche flat-sixes retained is the distance between the cylinder centres of 118mm. The engine has, however, benefited from the 33 years of development devoted to the units that have powered the Porsche 911 for both road use and racing, a career that culminated in the 16th Porsche victory at Le Mans in 1998.

THE ENGINE STRUCTURE

While the air-cooled engines had individual cylinders spigoted separately to the crankcase – so as to ensure the circulation of cooling air between the cylinders – in the liquid-cooled engines each group of three cylinders forms a single casting, as is also

the case for the cylinder heads, in the latter instance following the latest water-cooled racing engines. Blocks and heads are identical, and thus interchangeable, for both sides of the engine.

The cylinder blocks are an open-deck design. In contrast to the earlier engines however, the crankcase does not directly carry the seven crankshaft bearings. These are part of a longitudinally-split two-piece bearing block held in the crankcase by four long studs running horizontally around each cylinder, 12 in all on either side of the engine, these holding together, sandwich-fashion, the cam box, the cylinder head and one half of the bearing block.

▼ The M96/20 engine with transmission and exhaust system

The two parts of the bearing block are cast in aluminium alloy, as is the rest of the engine, but the thin-shell bearings are held in cast-iron supports incorporated in the bearing block. This avoids the drop in oil pressure and the increased operating noise that would otherwise be caused by the more rapid expansion of the aluminium, compared with the steel crankshaft, when the engine reaches a high temperature – thereby provoking an excessive increase in the main-bearing clearances. Oil jets incorporated in the bearing block ensure adequate cooling of the pistons as the oil pressure exceeds 26psi (1.8 bar).

The Boxster's M96/20 engine was the first in the world to use cylinder blocks produced by the 'Lokasil' process developed by the Kolbenschmidt (KS) company in cooperation with Porsche. This is more economical than either using a complete cylinder block cast in a highly wear-resistant aluminium alloy with a high silicon content, of which the bores must be treated by etching

▲ The engine and transmission package fits neatly into the rear of the car, still leaving space for luggage

▶ The two cylinder blocks and the cast-aluminium main-bearing block with cast-iron bearing inserts (arrows) of the M96/20 engine

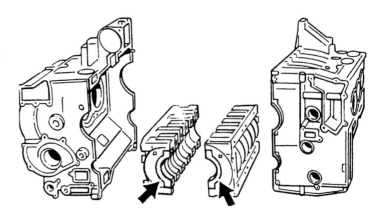

before machining, or the Nikasil process successfully used by Porsche for many years, which requires an expensive treatment after the casting process and is prone to corrosion by fuels with a high sulphur content.

▼ Power and torque curves of the 2.5-litre M96/20 Boxster engine

In the Lokasil process, the aluminium block is cast around highly porous silicon cylinder liners. The aluminium penetrates the pores in the liners, expelling the air to make a highly resistant

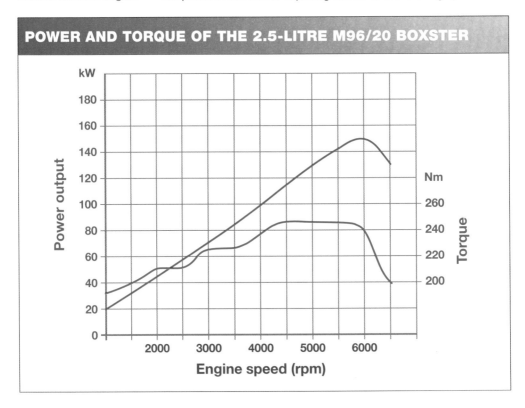

POWER AND TORQUE OF THE 2.5-LITRE M96/20 BOXSTER

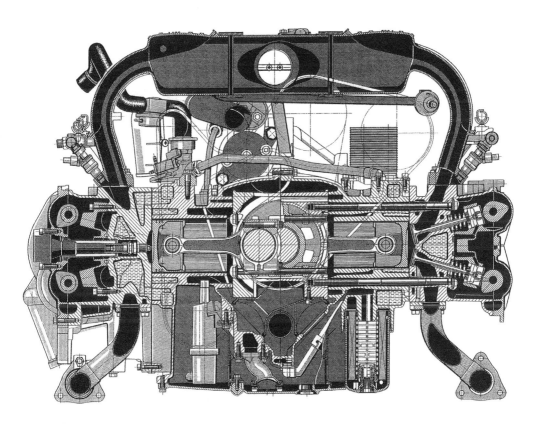

bore surface which holds oil well and does not require any further treatment before machining. To match the Lokasil bore surface, the high-pressure-cast aluminium-alloy pistons are iron-coated. They carry two compression rings and one oil scraper, and the gudgeon pin is offset by 0.8mm towards the intake side to equalise wear. The piston crown is partly recessed and the surround of the crown forms a squish zone with the overlapping edges of the cylinder head. The compression ratio is 11.0:1.

At first there were problems with porous Lokasil blocks, caused by too rapid a casting and cooling-down process. Engines found to suffer from this problem were immediately replaced without charge. Being the first of the two sister (Boxster and 911) engines to be put into production, the majority of faulty engines were among those powering Boxsters. The problem was solved by increasing manufacturing capacity at the KS factory and allowing the blocks to weather for longer before being machined.

The forged nitro-carbon-treated crankshaft carries 12 counterweights and a twin-mass flywheel. This is intended to filter the transmission to the gearbox of the irregular revolution speed of the crankshaft caused by the firing impulses, which induce

▲ Transverse cutaway view of the 2.5-litre M96/20 Boxster engine

noisy vibrations of the free-running gears and synchromesh at low engine speeds.

The twin-mass flywheel consists of two co-axial flywheels, a primary flywheel bolted to the crankshaft and a secondary flywheel running freely on a bearing that is part of the primary flywheel and is driven from it by circumferential springs. This allows a relative movement of about 50° between the two masses. The twin-mass flywheel forms a quite compact unit and carries a conventional clutch mechanism, driven by the secondary flywheel.

The front end of the crankshaft carries the sprocket driving the hollow 'intermediate' shaft at 0.666 times crankshaft speed by a duplex (twin-row) chain. Point welded to the flywheel is a sheet-metal disc with 60 peripheral teeth of which two are missing. The gap is registered by an inductive sensor and at each revolution of the crankshaft sends a signal to the Bosch Motronic 5.2.2 DME (engine management unit), which calculates the crankshaft rotating speed.

▼ The connecting rod caps are produced by 'cracking'

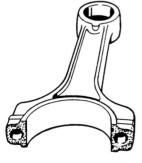

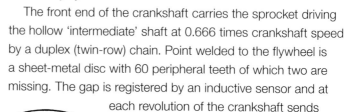

The connecting rods are forged in one piece with the complete big-end forming a ring which, after machining, is split by 'cracking'. This process consists in breaking the bearing cap away from the rod at two precisely marked points. This produces rough but intimately matching surfaces, different for every rod, and allows for the utmost precision of assembly. Porsche was the first engine manufacturer to apply the 'cracking' method to forged con-rods.

CYLINDER HEADS AND VALVE GEAR

The four-bearing hollow camshafts run in separate camboxes of which the upper bearing halves are an integral part. The camshafts operate two intake and two exhaust valves per cylinder through inverted cup tappets with zero-lash hydraulic adjustment. The intake valve diameter is 33.3mm and the exhaust valves are slightly smaller, with a diameter of 28.1mm. The included valve angle is 30° and the single valve springs are conical to avoid surge (which can lead to unpredictable spring

▲ The Boxster engine's nitro-carbon treated crankshaft has twelve counterweights and runs in seven bearings

behaviour at certain frequencies). Valve lift is 10mm on both intake and exhaust.

The camboxes and the cylinder heads are made of different aluminium alloys, the head being cast in a low-expansion alloy to keep the valve-seat inserts in place, while the camboxes in which the tappets operate are in a highly wear-resistant alloy. Another important reason for separating cambox and cylinder head is to avoid having external oil lines, always a possible cause of failure.

To achieve the desired left-to-right interchangeability of the principal castings and simultaneously to keep the engine as short as possible, Porsche has taken advantage of the offset of one cylinder bank to the other by driving the left-hand camshafts from the front of the block and the right-hand camshafts from the rear. The crankshaft thus carries at its rear a 24-tooth sprocket from which a short duplex chain drives the 36-tooth sprocket of a hollow intermediate shaft located under the crankshaft and extending over the entire length of the engine.

▶ **Cross section of the 2.5-litre Boxster engine's four-valve cylinder head, showing the very small valve angle resulting in a compact combustion chamber and the nearly-straight intake port (on left)**

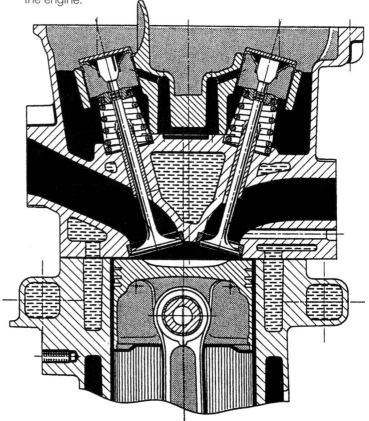

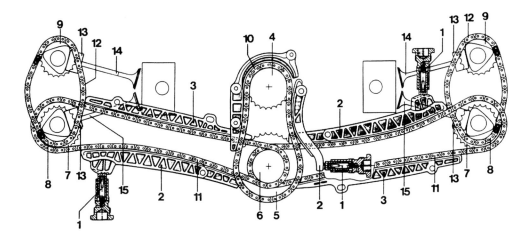

The intermediate shaft runs at 0.666 times crankshaft speed, and from each end a 21-tooth sprocket drives the 28-tooth sprockets of the exhaust camshafts by a duplex chain – controlled by a hydraulic tensioner in plastic material. The intake camshafts are in turn chain-driven from the exhaust camshafts, the drive incorporating a 'Variocam' cam-angle variator. The 'Variocam' modifies the intake camshaft timing to optimise the engine's torque curve and also helps meet emission targets.

At idle and up to 1,200rpm, the intake camshafts are in the late position, resulting in only a small overlap between the opening of the intake valves and the closing of the exhaust valves. This avoids a fresh charge escaping unburnt into the exhaust system and benefits smooth low-speed operation. Over 1,200rpm, the intake camshafts are advanced by 12.5°, which means that the intake valves open and close 25° earlier, measured on the crankshaft position. This earlier valve opening improves breathing and creates a certain amount of exhaust gas recirculation (EGR), thereby reducing the nitrogen oxide (NOx) emissions. The camshafts remain in this position until 5,120rpm is exceeded, when the intake camshafts return to their original position to benefit from the later closing of the intake valves after bottom dead centre and to exploit the high inertia of the fresh charge which helps it to continue streaming into the cylinder after the piston has reached bottom dead centre. This is more beneficial than an early intake valve opening.

The Variocam system is controlled by the Bosch Motronic 'Digital Motor Electronics' (or DME) engine-management system. A Hall sensor on the right-hand cylinder head faces a disc carried

▲ Timing Chains of the M96/20 2.5-litre engine:

1   Chain tensioner
2   Tensioning rail
3   Guiding rail
4   Crankshaft pinion, 24 teeth
5   Intermediate shaft pinion, 36 teeth
6   Intermediate shaft pinion, 21 teeth
7   Exhaust camshaft pinion, 28 teeth
8   Exhaust camshaft pinion, 21 teeth
9   Intake camshaft-driven pinion, 21 teeth
10 Duplex roller chain
11 Duplex roller chain
12 Simplex roller chain
13 Tappet
14 Intake valve
15 Exhaust valve

by the intake camshaft. The sensor registers the camshaft position and forwards the message to the DME, which is also informed of the crankshaft position by the flywheel sensor. From this data the DME calculates whether the intake camshafts are in the 'early' or 'late' position and adjusts ignition and injection timing to achieve the best possible performance and economy while meeting emission requirements. It is also a reference for the operation of the knock sensors.

THE TIMING DIAGRAM AT 1MM VALVE LIFT:

'Early' diagram: Intake   opens 11° before TDC
                              closes 19° after BDC

'Late' diagram: Intake   opens 14° after TDC
                              closes 44° after BDC

                    Exhaust   opens 39° before BDC
                              closes 8° before TDC

(TDC = Top Dead Centre, BDC = Bottom Dead Centre)

Note: According to the above figures, with the camshafts in the 'late' position, there is no overlap between the opening of the intake valves and the closing of the exhaust valves. This is due to the fact that the figures are given for 1mm valve opening, whereas when the engine is running, the clearance is down to zero, thanks to the hydraulic tappets.

COOLING

There is a single water pump integrated in the right-hand cylinder bank. The total coolant capacity is 18 litres, or 19 litres in cars with Tiptronic transmission. A full 70 per cent of the coolant penetrates the cylinder heads, in which it flows from the exhaust to the intake side to reduce temperature differences in the heads and thus avoid the risk of distortion. The cylinders take 20 per cent of the coolant and the remaining 10 per cent flows through the engine oil-cooler – and, if applicable, the Tiptronic heat-exchanger. A thermostat takes care of a quick engine warm-up and quick operation of the cabin heater. It is pressure sensitive and opens at a temperature of 87°C.

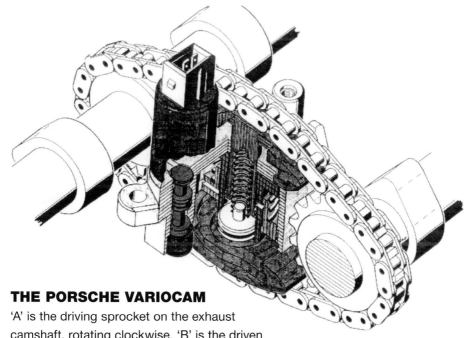

THE PORSCHE VARIOCAM

'A' is the driving sprocket on the exhaust
camshaft, rotating clockwise. 'B' is the driven
sprocket on the intake camshaft. The two sprockets are
linked by overlong chain 'C' – which for correct operation
must be tensioned, in this case by hydraulically-operated
and electronically-controlled double chain tensioner 'T'
located between the upper and lower chain links. On the
illustration the tensioner pulls the chain down. For a better
understanding, let us suppose that sprocket 'A' is immobile
and that hydraulic pressure moves the tensioner to push
the upper chain link up. In doing so it will turn the driven
sprocket 'B' clockwise, advancing the intake camshaft. If the
tensioner pushes the chain down, the operation is reversed.

▲ The chain
tensioner type
'Variocam' camshaft
angle variator

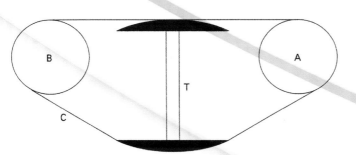

◀ Working principle
of the 'Variocam'
cam angle variator

▶ M96/20 engine
cooling system.

1 Water pump
2 Crankcase
3 Thermostat
4 Radiator
5 Cockpit heater
6 Engine oil/water
   heat exchanger
7 Tiptronic
   transmission oil/
   water heat exchanger
   (if applicable)
8 Electric shut-off valve
   (Tiptronic only)
9 Expansion reservoir
10 Shut-off valve
11 Engine breather
12 Radiator breather

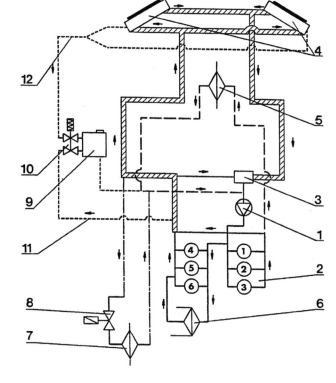

LUBRICATION

As in all Porsche models, engine lubrication is by the dry-sump system, but instead of being a separate entity, the 8.25-litre tank is part of the engine and mounted directly below the crankcase; oil thus returns to it by gravity, without the need for a special scavenge pump. Scavenge pumps are nevertheless necessary to return the oil from the cylinder heads to the tank.

▼ Oil scavenge pump.
This type of oil pump
is used to return the oil
from the cylinder heads
to the oil sump

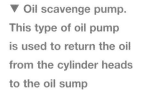

The oil is circulated by the pressure pump driven from the intermediate shaft. From the tank, the oil passes through the oil filter and thence to the oil/water heat-exchanger, from where it is fed to the main bearings and to the integrated piston-cooling jets. From there it proceeds to the cylinder heads, feeding the camshaft bearings and the hydraulic tappets. A separate high-pressure line feeds the Variocam chain tensioner. In each cylinder head a scavenge pump, driven by the exhaust camshaft, returns the oil to the 'swirlpot' air separator and thence to the oil tank. Separating any air from the oil is essential for the correct operation of the hydraulic

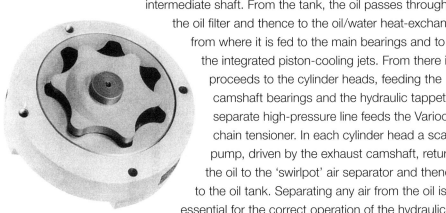

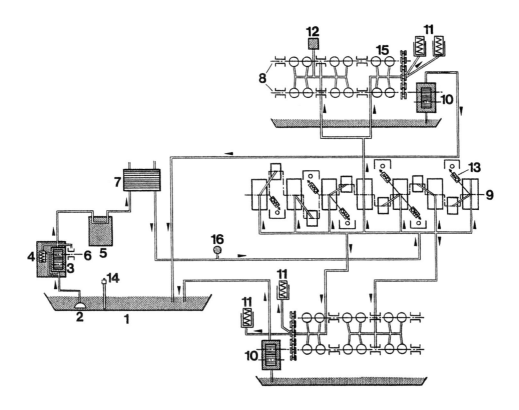

valve tappets. Rubber flap valves prevent air from being picked up by the pressure pump when the car experiences high or prolonged acceleration or cornering forces.

IGNITION AND FUEL SYSTEMS

The M96 engine family is the first in which Porsche uses a solid-state ignition system. From the signals received from the right bank intake camshaft-driven Hall sensor and the crankshaft speed sensor, from the throttle opening sensor and in consideration of various correcting factors such as air, water and oil temperature, the DME calculates the ignition timing for every single engine condition. It then distributes the 12 volt primary current of 7.5 amperes to the mini-coils on top of the six spark plugs. The coils raise the tension up to 28,000 volts for safe firing of the plugs. Since the cables leading to the mini-coils carry a current of only 12 volts, the risk of shorts caused by humidity or damaged cables is much reduced compared with cables carrying a current of several thousand volts.

The need for compactness led to the choice of an intake system similar in principle to that used successfully in the

▲ Lubricating circuit of M96/20 engine.

1 Oil pan
2 Oil intake
3 Oil pump
4 Oil pressure release valve
5 Full flow oil filter
6 Intermediate shaft
7 Oil/water heat exchanger
8 Camshafts
9 Crankshaft
10 Oil pressure pumps
11 Chain tensioner
12 Oil pressure sensor
13 Piston cooling jet valves
14 Oil level sensor
15 Hydraulic tappet
16 Oil temperature sensor

3.2-litre 911 of 1984–89. Cool air is drawn into the air filter housing by a 'schnorchel' in the left-hand body side, ahead of the rear wheelarch. The filter housing is carried by the side of the body and, after passing through the filter element, the air flows through the hot-film air mass meter integrated in the filter housing and through a flexible hose leading to the throttle-valve unit. This incorporates an idle-speed stabiliser controlled by the DME and a potentiometer measuring the throttle valve angle. Just before the throttle valve there is a Helmholtz resonator to produce a pleasant, 'sporty' intake sound. Downstream of the throttle valve the intake air is led to a transverse pipe feeding the two plenum chambers, each of which feeds three cylinders.

The intake system is made entirely of plastic, which not only saves weight but also ensures perfectly smooth internal surfaces. Only the throttle-valve unit is metallic.

Except for the higher-performance Bosch Motronic 5.2.2 DME, the injection system is very similar to the one used in the 993-series 911 and is identical to the system used in the 996-series 911. An active carbon tank located in the right front wheel

▼ Air intake system. The intake air flows through the air filter and air mass meter (1) and proceeds through the plastic pipe (2) to the throttle body (3). A silencer (4) is connected to the air pipe and creates resonances which reduce the intake roar

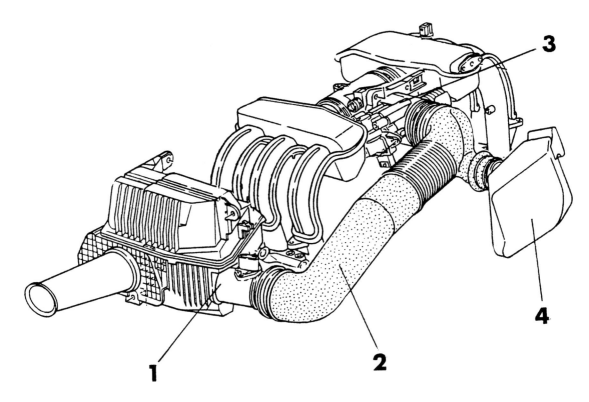

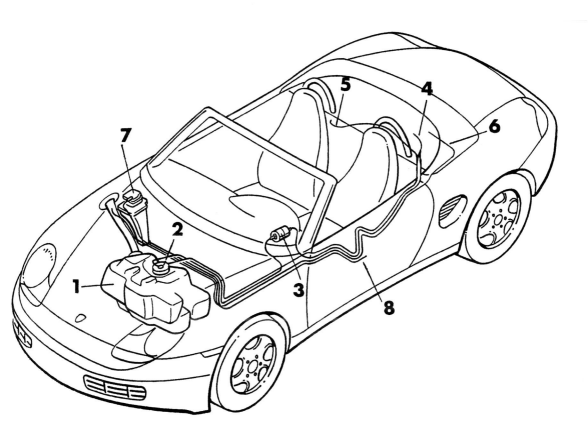

▲ Fuel System of the
Boxster (1997–2000).

housing absorbs the fuel fumes forming in the tank when the car is stationary. As the engine is started, the fumes are fed into the intake system and a ventilator regenerates the active carbon with fresh air.

The fuel pump is immersed in the 60 litre tank and the injection system incorporates a pressure limiter keeping the operating pressure at 55+3psi (3.8+0.2bar). The quantity of fuel injected into the intake ports by the solenoid-operated injectors depends on the time the injectors remain open. It is monitored by the DME, which integrates the signals received from the air mass sensor, corrected as necessary by an intake air temperature sensor as well as from other sources. Any surplus fuel reaching the injectors is returned to the tank.

The air-mass sensor consists of an electrical bridge circuit installed on a ceramic substrate in the form of thin film resistors. The sensor is integrated in the air filter housing, downstream of the filter element in such a way that the film is protected from dirt. In 160,000km (approx. 100,000 miles) the film efficiency is reduced by only three per cent. The film is divided into three zones; the central zone which is electrically-heated to a high

1 Fuel tank
2 Fuel pipe with in-tank
   pump and fuel level
   sensor
3 Fuel filter
4 Fuel arrival
5 Fuel return pipe
6 Line to active carbon
   container
7 Active carbon
   container
8 Scavenge line

◢ Air mass sensor. At the top of the drawing, the sensor is turned as it is exposed to the air stream when it leaves the air filter. In the bottom drawing the sensor is turned 90°, showing the path of the air (1) through the sensor (dotted line). The air returns to the main stream in (3) after being heated by the hot film (2). The hot film is divided in three zones: the central zone which is electrically heated at a temperature kept constant by the DME, and two temperature metering zones, one upstream and one downstream of the heated central zone. The air temperature difference between the two zones is a measure of the mass of air aspirated by the engine

temperature and kept constant by a closed circuit in the DME, and two temperature metering zones, one upstream and the other downstream of the heated zone. The temperature difference between the two zones is a measure of the mass of air aspirated by the engine, from which the DME calculates the amount of fuel to be injected to achieve an air/fuel mass ratio of Lambda 1 for optimal catalyst efficiency, taking into account such data as intake air temperature, coolant and oil temperature. The lowest specific

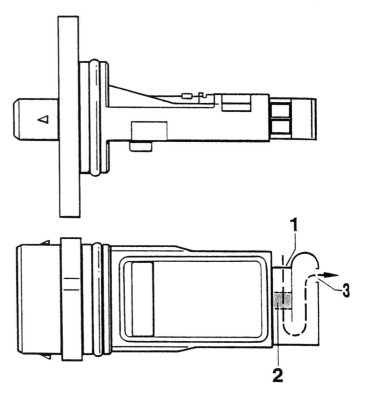

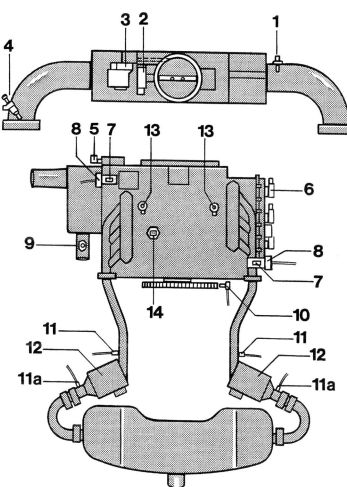

◀ Schematic diagram of DME (electronic engine management).

1 Intake temperature sensor
2 Throttle potentiometer
3 Idle speed regulator
4 Fuel injector
5 Engine temperature sensor
6 Ignition coil
7 Hall captor
8 Variocam control valve
9 Air mass meter
10 Engine speed sensor
11 Lambda sensor
11a Lambda sensor (USA only)
12 Catalyst
13 Knock sensor
14 Oil temperature sensor

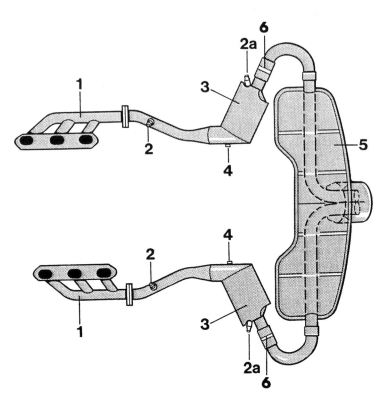

► Exhaust system of
the Boxster 2.5 litre.
1   Exhaust manifolds
2   Lambda (oxygen)
    sensor
3   Metal core catalyst
4   Screw connection
    for exhaust gas
    analysis
5   Common tail
    silencer
6   Pipe connection
2a Lambda sensor
    (USA cars only,
    worldwide from
    model year 2000)

fuel consumption of 240g per kW/h (176g per bhp/h) is obtained
between 3,000 and 3,600rpm for a mean effective pressure of
9.8bar. The maximum bmep (brake mean effective pressure)
of 12.2bar is obtained between 4,500 and 5,500rpm.

Two knock sensors, one per cylinder bank, screwed to
the bottom of the central cylinder, protect the engine against
detonation which can develop for various reasons, such as the
use of a fuel of less than 98 RON rating. The sensors send the
knock signal to the DME which retards the ignition in steps of
2.25° until the knock disappears, up to 15° if necessary, after which
the normal ignition timing is progressively restored. Each bank
of cylinders has its own three branch high quality steel exhaust
manifold merging into a pipe leading to the platinum-rhodium
metallic core three-way catalyst and into a common, transverse-
mounted silencer with central tail pipe. The silencer is a double-
skinned rustproof steel unit. It is rigidly bolted to the gearbox
because the entire rubber mounted engine, gearbox and exhaust
unit is used as a vibration damper for the entire car structure.

A 'Lambda' oxygen sensor analyses the exhaust gases before
they reach the catalyst. A too-high or too-low oxygen content of

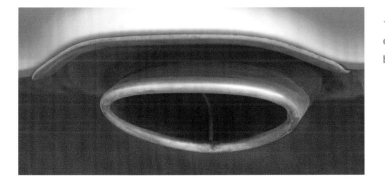

◄ An oval tail pipe is characteristic of the basic Boxster

the gases translates into an electric current advising the DME to modify the air/fuel ratio accordingly. An additional Lambda sensor is fitted downstream of the catalyst to cars for export to the United States to meet OBD II requirements. It checks the gases after the catalytic treatment and a warning light is activated in the case of an anomaly. Cars for Europe have been similarly equipped from model year 2000, when the engines were tuned to meet the Euro 3 and the stricter German D4 exhaust emission standards.

▼ The air intakes in the front skirt feed the twin radiators and the front brakes

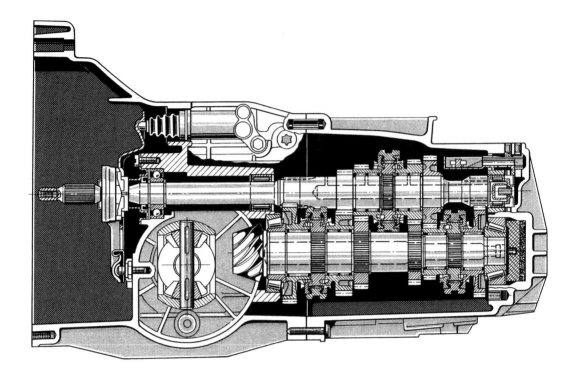

▲ The Boxster's
G86/00 five-speed
manual gearbox
incorporating the final
drive and differential

THE TRANSMISSION

The standard transmission of the Boxster, as it was introduced
in 1996, consists of a five-speed gearbox and differential unit,
and is not related to either the G50 gearbox of the 964/993-
series 911 models or their 996 successor. A ZF-made five-speed
automatic transmission with sequential manual shift facility was
available as an option, and was the first five-speed automatic
offered in a Porsche car.

THE 5-SPEED G86/00 MANUAL GEARBOX

The gearbox overhangs the rear axle and is operated from the
gear lever by cables to avoid any 'telegraphing' of gear noises
into the cockpit. A hydraulically operated single-plate pulled
diaphragm-spring clutch bolted to the twin-mass flywheel drives
the gearbox primary (input) shaft located above the secondary
(output) shaft, taking the drive to the differential located between
the clutch and the gearbox. The clutch and differential housing
form one single part to which the gearbox housing is bolted. Both
are in aluminium. The gearbox is filled with 2.5 litres of a special
lubricant, which only requires changing after 100,000 miles.

GEAR RATIOS – MANUAL

Gear	Gear teeth pairing	Output: input ratio	mph at 1,000rpm with 225/50 R16 tyres
1st	10/35	3.500	5.3
2nd	17/36	2.118	8.8
3rd	28/40	1.429	12.9
4th	34/35	1.029	18.0
5th	38/30	0.789	23.4
Reverse		3.440	
Final drive	9/35	3.889	

▲ G86/00 gearbox of the 2.5-litre Boxster. The G86/01 gearbox of the 2.7-litre model (from model year 2000) differs only by the internal ratios

▲ A86/00 Tiptronic transmission of the 2.5-litre Boxster. Externally, the unit of the 2.7-litre model is identical

GEAR RATIOS – TIPTRONIC

Gear	Ratio
1st	3.67: 1
2nd	2.00: 1
3rd	1.41: 1
4th	1.00: 1
5th	0.74: 1
Reverse	4.10: 1

Final gear set 24/41/30 = 1.25:1
Final drive: 4.205:1
Crown wheel/pinion: 3.364:1
Speed in top gear at 1,000 rpm = 23.4mph

Torque converter
Diameter: 254mm
Multiplication factor: 1.98
Stall speed: 2,400 rpm

THE A86/00 TIPTRONIC GEARBOX

The hardware of the optional Tiptronic S transmission is a conventional five-speed and reverse epicyclic gear transmission with hydrodynamic torque converter and wet single-plate converter lock-up clutch. The lock-up clutch establishes a direct mechanical drive from the engine flywheel to the gearbox input shaft, bypassing the torque converter when the engine speed reaches a level at which the torque multiplication in the converter ceases. From that point on, the torque converter can only act as a hydrodynamic coupling transmitting the torque with a slip of approximately three per cent and an equivalent loss of efficiency, which the lock-up clutch avoids. The converter lock-up also provides a more spontaneous and sporting throttle response, similar to that provided by a manual transmission.

However, bypassing the torque converter has a disadvantage in that the transmission no longer benefits from the 'cushion' effect of the hydraulic converter, which prevents the irregular crankshaft speed – inevitable in a reciprocating engine – from causing audible vibrations of the gear set. Hence, between the 'clutch open' and 'clutch closed' modes, a third mode of 'controlled slip' is used to largely preserve the advantage of the complete lock-up while obtaining a smoother transition and quieter operation. The operating mode of the lock-up clutch is as follows:

1st gear: Always open

2nd gear: Up to 15mph: open; 18–22mph: controlled slip: over 22mph: closed

3rd gear: Up to 15mph: open; 18–30mph: controlled slip: over 30mph: closed

4th gear: Up to 22 mph: open; 23–30mph: controlled slip: over 30mph: closed

5th gear: Up to 27 mph: open; 30–36mph: controlled slip: over 36mph: closed

The 'controlled slip' mode is also automatically selected for a smoother transition when shifting down on the overrun.

The automatic mode of the gearbox is obtained with the selector lever in the 'D' position, the manual sequential mode by moving the selector lever to the 'M' position. The manual shifts are controlled by fingertip toggle switches on the steering wheel. The selector lever and the switches communicate electrically with the Tiptronic Control Unit located in the rear luggage compartment. This in turn communicates with the DME module to ensure the quickest and smoothest possible shifts.

In the 'D' (automatic) position of the selector lever the Tiptronic control unit chooses from five shift programmes the most appropriate for the prevailing driving conditions. The first programme corresponds to a quiet, leisurely driving style, the fifth programme to a fast and enterprising style. The driving style is recognised by the control unit by the speed at which the accelerator pedal is operated, the opening angle of the throttle valve and the accelerations and decelerations of the vehicle. Large throttle pedal movements rapidly call up a sportier programme with later automatic upshifts and earlier downshifts.

Whatever the programme, quickly lifting off the accelerator prevents an automatic up-shift, for example when coming up to a bend, while automatic up and down shifts are prevented during cornering where lateral acceleration exceeds 0.5g to avoid destabilising the car.

On a gradient the shift points are automatically raised on any programme and hard braking produces an early down-shift, which can be useful for the forthcoming acceleration or downhill for engine braking.

The programme calculated by the Tiptronic Control Unit is implemented by the Electro-Valve Unit of the gearbox, which also controls the pressure of the hydraulic system as a function of the power requirement of the various gear selection, brakes and clutches, so as to avoid unnecessary power absorption. Thanks to the interaction between the Tiptronic Control Unit and the DME, very smooth gear changes are obtained by the reduction

▼ Components of the torque converter of the A86/00 transmission. From left: Converter overriding clutch (two pieces); torque converter wheel; pump wheel with 'free wheel' mounted stator

of the throttle valve opening for the duration of the shift and by allowing a slight slip of the lock-up clutch during a down shift.

In the manual mode the driver selects the gears using the toggle switches on the steering wheel. However, to save the engine from overrevving, a lower gear can only be selected if it is compatible with the car's speed. And even in the manual mode, the transmission automatically shifts into a lower gear if the car's speed becomes too low for the engine to pull cleanly. If the car comes to rest, second gear is automatically engaged to allow a smooth restart. If the driver prefers starting in first gear for a quicker getaway, he can select first or floor the accelerator to operate the kick-down.

An oil/water heat exchanger is bolted to the Tiptronic gearbox casing; coolant temperature is controlled by a vacuum-operated valve which opens when the gearbox oil temperature exceeds 85°C or the water temperature exceeds 90°C.

The Tiptronic unit weighs approximately 107kg and adds 50kg to the car's weight, compared with the manual transmission. It contains nine litres of special ATM lubricant which only requires changing after 100,000 miles.

▲ The four-spoke steering wheel typical of 1997–1999 models, here with Tiptronic S trigger switches

CHAPTER 3

Running gear, steering and driving aids

Both the Boxster and the 996-series 911 use similar front suspension and running gear, except for such model-specific items as the size of the brakes and the wheels.

During development, the most important requirements for the Boxster's running gear were identified as the following:

- Very high driving safety under all conditions and whatever the weight carried
- Very high transverse acceleration
- Safe and consistent behaviour when changing lane at any speed
- Easily controllable lift-off reaction when cornering
- Low steering effort
- Small roll and pitch angles when cornering and when braking to provide a feel of agility and response

These requirements were not to interfere with:
- Really good comfort in all circumstances;
- Low road noise and vibration level; and
- Avoidance of driver tiredness when driving over long distances

Shared with the front end of the 911 are all the suspension arms, the wheel carriers and the double-T shaped crossmember carrying the steering gear and on which the suspension arms are pivoted. All these cast parts are in various types of aluminium alloy. Only the model-specific parts, such as the springs, the damper internals, the anti-roll bar thicknesses and the brakes, are unique to the Boxster.

The Boxster goes one step further by using identical suspension units front and rear, the rear suspension, except for the longitudinal arms, being the same as the front suspension but turned through 180° (the 911 uses a multi-link rear suspension because of its greater rear weight bias). In the Boxster, front and rear suspensions differ only by the length of

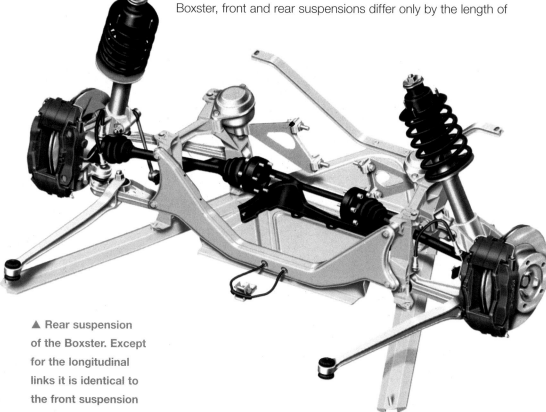

▲ Rear suspension of the Boxster. Except for the longitudinal links it is identical to the front suspension

the longitudinal arms and the shape of the crossmember on which the suspension arms are pivoted. The crossmember is bolted to a rigidly mounted subframe, which is an important part of the body structure, and at its upper ends directly to the body itself.

The much-modified McPherson-type strut suspension was chosen for a number of reasons: it provides good fore-and-aft compliance, therefore reducing harshness but without inducing excessive caster variations; intrusion into the front and rear luggage compartments is limited; it responds well to small inputs from the road, ensuring low-speed comfort; the crossmember can be integrated into the car structure to absorb energy in frontal and rear crashes; and the entire suspension can be built as a self-contained module. The small number of parts and light weight of strut suspension were also important factors.

On either side, the suspension arm is pivoted at its inner end on a rubber bushing, which is very stiff radially. The longitudinal link, which extends forward, forms a triangle with the arm and is mounted with soft bushes at either end to allow the required fore-and-aft compliance.

▲ **Front suspension, steering and brakes of the 2.5-litre and 2.7-litre Boxster, seen from the front**

▲ Rear view of the rear suspension, brakes and subframe of the 2.5-litre and 2.7-litre models

In the rear suspension, toe-in is controlled by a ball-jointed track rod, which takes the place of the steering track rod in the front suspension but is pivoted on the subframe behind the wheel axis. Toe-in increases as the suspension is compressed, so as to create understeer by increasing the toe-in of the outer rear wheel when cornering. This has little effect on steady cornering, but stabilises the car when turning-in or changing lane at speed.

The coil springs are conical to reduce their length; they are also not concentric with the strut, which reduces the bending moment on the strut when compressed and the resultant friction of the damper rod on the strut body formed by the twin tube, gas-filled damper. The anti-roll bar is directly connected to the strut by a ball-jointed link for immediate response. In the top mounting of the strut, two separate rubber cushions are used for the spring and the damper rod to avoid pre-compressing the damper rod mounting rubber with the forces permanently exerted by the spring.

From the beginning of its career, the Boxster was available with a harder 'sport' suspension in conjunction with wider 17in wheels – these also being available as an option with the standard suspension. The 'sport' suspension includes a 10mm lower ride height, harder springs, stiffer anti-roll bars and harder dampers.

In view of the fact that under certain circumstances, the ABS function can cause one of the front wheels to be braked harder than the other, trying to turn the car off its proposed line, the front wheels have a negative offset at the ground of 7mm (with 16in wheels and with the 18in wheels which became an option in 1998) to pull the steering in the opposite direction. The rim offset of the 17in front wheels being 5mm greater, in this instance the negative offset at the ground is increased by 12mm.

Pitching movements caused by positive and negative acceleration and by driving and braking torques are opposed by the anti-dive and anti-squat geometry of the front and rear suspensions respectively. The vertical inertia force required to correct the pitching movements can be engineered into the caster angle of the front struts and of the location of the pivot points for the longitudinal links. Unfortunately this would conflict with the need for fore-and-aft compliance of the suspension. For this reason most of the anti-dive and anti-squat work is left to the rear

RUNNING GEAR SPECIFICATIONS

	Front	Rear
Roll centre height	76mm	76mm
Track (16in wheels)	1,465mm	1,528mm
Track (17in wheels)	1,455mm	1,508mm
Wheels	6J 16 H2 RO 50*	7J 16 H2 RO 40*
Wheels (sport)	7J 17 H2 RO 55	8.5J 17 H2 RO 50
Tyres	205/55 ZR 16	225/50 ZR 16
Tyres (sport)	205/50 ZR 17	255/40 ZR 17
Spring rate at wheel	24N/mm	27N/mm
Anti-roll bar (tubular)		
Diameter x Thickness	23.1 x 3.4mm	18.5 x 2.5mm
Anti-roll bar (sport)	23.5 x 3.5mm	19.6 x 2.6mm
Dampers	Twin-tube, gas filled	Twin-tube, gas filled
Weight on axle	585kg	665kg
Weight on axle (sport)	590kg	675kg
Weight distribution	47.8%	52.2%
Weight distribution (sport)	46.6%	53.4%
(*RO = Offset of the wheel rim vertical axis to the hub flange plane)		

▶ Front brake with monobloc aluminium calliper of the 2.5-litre and 2.7-litre Boxster

suspension where this conflict does not exist. While the front suspension compensates the dive forces by only 11 per cent, rear anti-dive amounts to 50 per cent and anti-squat to 91 per cent.

STEERING

The Boxster was the first Porsche to be fitted with an adjustable steering column, but for reach only, the adjustment range being 44mm. The steering column shafts transmit movement from the steering wheel to the hydraulically-assisted rack-and-pinion steering gear by means of an angled intermediate shaft. This carries a universal joint at either end and includes a deformable aluminium 'harmonica', which, together with the intermediate shaft angle, should ensure that the steering column does not move back into the cockpit in a frontal crash.

For better compatibility with the front suspension kinematics, the aluminium steering gear housing is located ahead of the front wheel axis. It is rigidly bolted to the front transverse member, the only elasticity introduced in the steering gear being the hard rubber joint on the steering pinion shaft. The linear hydraulic power assistance is provided by a pump, driven from the front end of the crankshaft by a multi-V belt. The steering ratio is 16.9:1 and the turning circle is 10.9m.

BRAKES

In consideration of the fact that some owners may want to take part in club racing events or take their car to 'track days' to enjoy its performance and handling safely and legally, the Boxster's brakes by far surpass the requirements of normal road use. They have been developed to meet the extreme requirements of the standard Porsche Brake Test. This consists of 25 consecutive retardations with a deceleration of 0.8g from 90 per cent of the car's maximum speed down to 100km/h (62mph) from where the car is immediately re-accelerated as quickly as possible, using the gearbox, to 90 per cent of its maximum speed, and so forth. During the entire test procedure the deceleration must never fall below 0.8g and the temperature of the discs must never exceed 700°C.

The brakes of the Boxster are operated by a twin circuit in which the tandem master cylinder is operated by a 10in diameter

vacuum servo, mounted on the dash structure. The mechanically-operated master cylinder piston operates the front wheel circuit and the floating piston operates the rear wheel circuit in which a pressure-limiting valve is integrated upstream of the Anti-lock Braking System (ABS) unit. The three-channel ABS operates separately on the front brakes and using the 'select low' principle on the rear brakes, where it operates on both brakes as soon as one rear wheel tends to lock.

The Boxster was the first production car to use aluminium monobloc brake callipers, as used in Porsche racing cars for some years. Previously, for easier manufacturing, the fixed calliper was made of two halves bolted together. The advantages of the monobloc callipers are

▼ Three-channel ABS
(standard on Boxster
2.5 litre).
1 ABS control unit
2 Tandem master
  cylinder
3 ABS hydraulic unit
4 ABS sensors
5 Central informator
6 Brake force limiter
7 Stop light
8 Stop light switch
9 ABS warning light

Both Diagrams
A Front brake circuit
B Rear brake circuit
C Hand brake cable
  guiding block

greater stiffness and lower weight, and their increased stiffness produces a firm pedal feel.

In the Boxster, four-piston monobloc callipers are used front and rear. Pistons of 36mm and 40mm diameter operate in the front callipers; pistons of 28mm and 30mm diameter are used at the rear, where the centre of the disc is a drum containing the two leading-shoe system of the cable-operated parking brakes. A pad wear warning light is included in the dashboard instruments.

All four cast-iron brake discs are ventilated by curved internal vanes. The front discs have a diameter of 298mm and are 24mm thick; the rear discs are 282mm by 20mm. Additional cooling air is directed to the front discs from the intakes in the front skirt by plastic ducting plates carried by the longitudinal suspension arms.

While ABS was standard equipment on early Boxsters, Traction Control (TC) combined with differential slip control (ABD) with individual anti-lock for all four wheels (four-channel ABS) was an option. A switch gives the driver the opportunity to choose between TC alone or in combination with ABD.

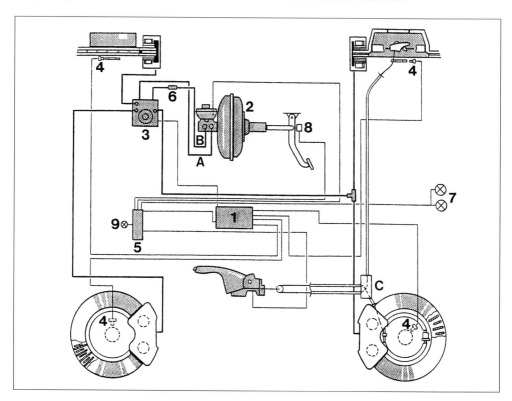

TC and ABD use the ABS wheel sensors to detect spin of one of the driving wheels. The spin indicates that the maximum driving force produced by the spinning wheel has been reached. Due to the differential, the driving force of the opposite wheel, which may be on a surface offering a better grip, is limited to the same driving force. Therefore the detected spin is communicated to the ABD control unit, which in turn applies the brake of the spinning wheel to check the spin and allow more torque to be transmitted through the differential to the opposite wheel and exploit its better grip. The end result is the same or better than with a conventional limited-slip differential, but the main advantage is that under all normal conditions the differential is completely free to function as intended.

If, despite the brake intervention on the spinning wheel, both driving wheels start spinning, the engine management system reduces the torque output of the engine by retarding the ignition. A warning light always informs the driver of any intervention of the TC or ABD. If necessary the system can be switched off, but for safety reasons it is reactivated every time the ignition switch is turned on.

▼ Four-channel ABS + TC function (optional on Boxster 2.5 litre).
1 ABS control unit
2 Tandem master cylinder
3 ABS hydraulic unit
4 ABS sensors
5 Central informator
6 Brake force limiter
7 Stop light
8 Stop light switch
9 ABS warning light
10 Traction control (TC) warning light
11 TC function light
12 DME engine management unit

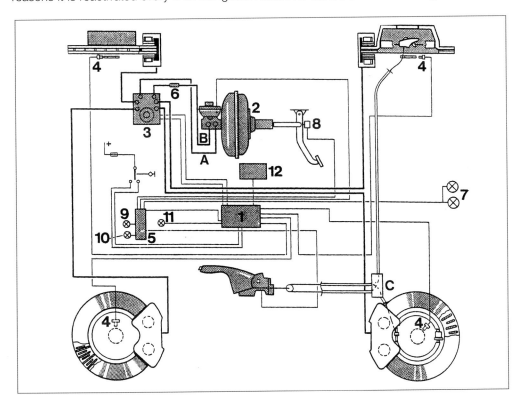

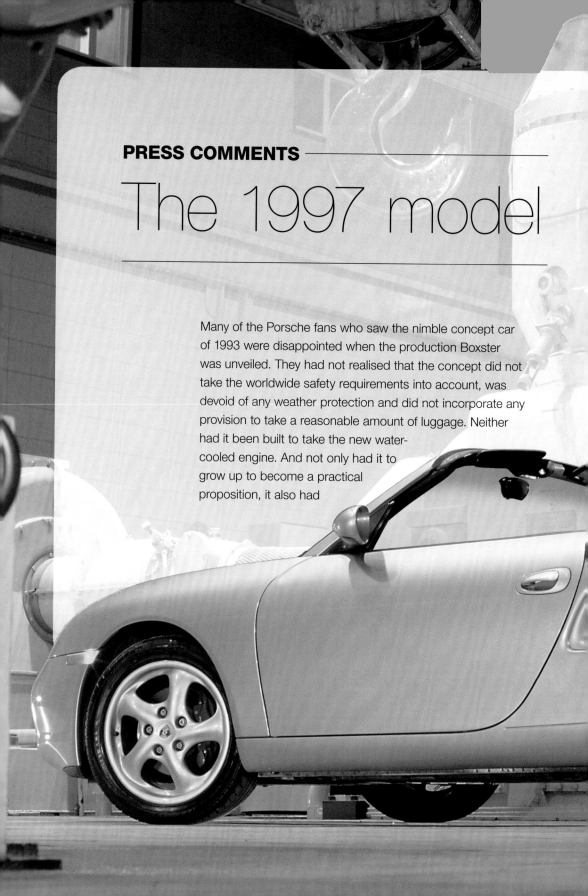

The 1997 model

Many of the Porsche fans who saw the nimble concept car of 1993 were disappointed when the production Boxster was unveiled. They had not realised that the concept did not take the worldwide safety requirements into account, was devoid of any weather protection and did not incorporate any provision to take a reasonable amount of luggage. Neither had it been built to take the new water-cooled engine. And not only had it to grow up to become a practical proposition, it also had

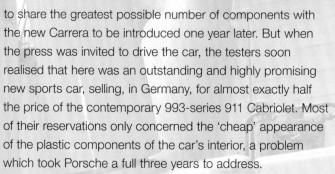

to share the greatest possible number of components with the new Carrera to be introduced one year later. But when the press was invited to drive the car, the testers soon realised that here was an outstanding and highly promising new sports car, selling, in Germany, for almost exactly half the price of the contemporary 993-series 911 Cabriolet. Most of their reservations only concerned the 'cheap' appearance of the plastic components of the car's interior, a problem which took Porsche a full three years to address.

This did not prevent the Boxster from becoming an instant bestseller and, except for two moderate power increases and a progressively improved quality of interior trim, it remained virtually unchanged for eight years. Though it was designed to be an entry-level model, it was never a cheap car. However, remembering that the entire front half of the car, including all the mechanical units it contains, and the engine (except for its slightly smaller capacity) were all but basically identical to the nearly twice-as-expensive 911's, the Boxster offered immense value.

▼ *Autocar*'s January 1997 road test praised the Boxster for its handling and powertrain, and commented that the flat-six engine 'loves to be used hard'. The cabin design was rated slightly disappointing although the ergonomics and hood won approval. Overall it was felt that the Boxster was the most important car for Porsche since the 924

WHAT THE PRESS SAID

In its 22 October 1996 issue, *Auto Motor und Sport*, Germany's leading motoring magazine wrote: "The new and classic six-cylinder engine is a dream. Water instead of air cooling has enhanced its refinement, but the acoustic talent with which its power is developed has not been lost. It extends from 'piano capricioso' at idle to 'fortissimo furioso' at 6,700rpm where the rev limiter puts a premature end to the acoustic delight... Under 3,000rpm the 2.5-litre engine responds keenly, but more is required before the flat-six unit really wakes up to life and it takes just short of 5,000rpm for the 204PS unit to really shine."

Concerning handling and comfort, the tester further commented: "Considering active safety, handling and suspension comfort, the chassis of the Boxster sets new benchmarks."

In its following issue (31 October 1996), *Auto Motor und Sport* published a comparative test of the Boxster and the contemporary series 1 Mercedes-Benz SLK 230 Kompressor. Except for the higher maximum speed of the Porsche (149mph against 143mph), the two cars displayed almost identical performance, but, the

▼ Even with the standard suspension there is very little roll when cornering fast

tester noted, "The Boxster does not succeed in exploiting its higher power for superior performance and the flexibility of its atmospheric engine is clearly inferior to the Mercedes' supercharger engine. But the water-cooled flat-six displays a really sporting character, responding sharply to accelerator inputs, revving turbine-smoothly, emitting the most Porsche-typical roar as soon as 5,000rpm are reached... For refinement the Mercedes' engine, good as it is for a four-cylinder, has no chance against the Boxster's flat-six."

But in the end, the SLK won the contest by a minimal margin, mainly because of its better mid-range torque, better ventilation and lower price.

The Boxster was also beaten – into third place – in a three-car comparison test published in the American magazine *Road & Track* (September 1999), just before the Boxster 2.7 was announced. A Boxster 2.5 was matched against a Honda 2000 roadster, which won the contest, and a BMW M roadster in 240PS American guise. The Boxster earned the highest marks for handling, steering, luggage space and soft top operation. It tied with the Honda in the braking department and was fastest

▲ Cockpit of the
manual Boxster
tested by *Autocar*

in the slalom. But its comparative lack of power made it the
slowest car on a lap of the Talladega race track (BMW 72.3sec,
Honda 73.8sec, Boxster 75.2sec).

In its 8 January 1997 road test, *Autocar*, the leading British
car magazine, recalls the 1993 'concept Boxster' commenting:
"The tension and poise that made the original motionless
Boxster scream 'buy me!' three years ago have gone, lost
along with its petite dimensions in the translation from concept
to production. Where the concept car had taut 550 Spyder-
inspired curves and exquisite proportions, the production
version gets bland, slab-sided and – thanks to golf-friendly
front and rear luggage compartments – uncomfortably
long overhangs."

However, the test report is much kinder to the power train
and the way the car handles: "The Boxster's low 1,242kg
weight is a big help to performance achieved through extensive
use of aluminium and other alloys. The engine's love of revs is
combined with a slick and precise five-speed transaxle. The
only complaint is that the gap between second and third gears
is too wide. You change gear for the fun of it in the Boxster,

and this gap mars it. Even heel-and-toeing when changing into second fails to disguise this gap. What's really needed is a six-speeder." A little further down, the test report goes on: "Porsche couldn't fit its double wishbone suspension to the Boxster for packaging reasons, so instead the car uses McPherson struts at both ends. They do a brilliant job. First surprise is how well it rides. This car has the optional 17 inch wheels and wider 255/45 rear tyres, but not the sport suspension package. Word is that the optional set-up is stiff enough to give more precision, but the standard car's compliant ride isn't sacrificed along with it... The car has no bad habits worth mentioning. Lifting off or braking in mid-corner – both motions that carry a stern warning in a 911 – do little to upset the Boxster. Even the 968 Club Sport doesn't feel as secure as this new Porsche."

A month after testing the manual shift Boxster, *Autocar* tested the Tiptronic version and commented: "Other than a small 50kg increase in kerb weight due to the extra gearbox gubbins, there are few significant differences between Tiptronic and manual Boxsters." The analysis continues with: "Porsche has ensured that all gears end up slightly lower in order that acceleration be kept on a par with the manual. It's a good effort in theory, but in practice the Tiptronic lacks much of the urgency and the involvement of the DIY version, despite the wheel-mounted push-button shifters." The report concludes: "Ultimately however, the fact that Tiptronic will override what it takes to be an inappropriate command is, ironically, the limiting factor in its appeal among the true enthusiasts. This, plus the fact that there is still a small but significant delay between pressing the shift buttons and the next gear actually engaging. There is also a marked drop-off in straight line performance, the Tiptronic's 0 to 60mph time rising to 7.3 seconds (from 6.5 seconds) along with the 0–100mph time (up by over a second to 19.1seconds). Top speed has also dropped to 136mph."

In the American magazine *Car & Driver* of November 1996, Peter Robinson, who obviously had the privilege of driving the Boxster before the start of the official press tests, was suitably impressed. "See the car in the flesh, and it tells you that the (1993) show car hasn't been compromised. Yes, it is 7.9

▼ A deep front boot gives 130 litres of luggage space

inches longer (all in the overhangs) than the show car, also 1.5 inches wider and a tad higher, but the benefit of a fabric top that retracts in 12 seconds at the push of a button – plus the sensibly large luggage compartments – can't be denied. Nor can a roomy cockpit with the driver's seat, the steering wheel and the pedals all in perfect alignment – something no previous Porsche has ever achieved.

"But where the Boxster really needed to deliver was on the road. It does brilliantly. At first the messages are confusing. Driving away from the Weissach development centre in Germany, we found the Boxster subdued, relaxed and refined. It doesn't sound like a Porsche. At least not yet. Only a long and clumsy clutch travel spoils the perception of civility and the throttle lacks the instant responsiveness of the 968. The new engine, always tractable and silky smooth, is at its best between 4,000 and the 6,600rpm red line."

Later in this article he comments: "Performance-wise the Boxster easily outshines BMW's new Z3 and the Benz SLK, though its appeal goes way beyond the claimed 6.7 seconds 0–60 time (7.4 for the Boxster equipped with the 5-speed

▲ When retracted, the rear spoiler is virtually unnoticeable

Tiptronic) and 149mph top speed with the manual." On the suspension he writes: "The suspension is taut, but it still delivers a quiet and comfortable ride. It feels nimble, responsive and agile – as expected in a mid-engined car – but it is also stable and predictable up to and at the very high limits of adhesion."

And he concludes: "The Boxster represents a return to the company's original philosophies wrapped in an entirely contemporary design. No other roadster offers the same blend of performance, handling, ride and refinement. Yes, it is dynamically superior to the 911 (993), though it is not as quick."

In the American *Car* magazine of October 1996, the well-known German writer Georg Kacher stated: "There is not a lot wrong with the basic attitude of the Boxster engine. Its power output betters that of most 2.5-litre engines, and the eagerness to rev keeps a smile on the driver's face. But in the end it just whets our appetite without appeasing the hunger... And the performance in the crucial 45–90mph range isn't

▼ **This action shot shows the flowing lines of the Boxster at their best**

sufficiently explosive." Further down the long article, Kacher continues: "The brakes are near perfect, the steering is another highlight. The Boxster's new underpinnings are just terrific." And he concludes: "A Porsche should never be short of poke – especially one that has such great brakes and steering."

In a comparative test between a Boxster and a Mercedes-Benz SLK, John Barker, writing for *Car* magazine of January 1997, concludes his article: "For now the Boxster is the driver's choice. It is special in many respects: the consistency and the weighting of its controls and the meatiness of its demeanour is everything you'd hope for in a Porsche. Yet somehow, given that it has the optimum layout for a sports car, I'd expected more. In naked dynamic terms, the Boxster isn't an exceptional mid-engined car like the Lotus Elise or the Honda NSX. But then Porsche isn't known for getting cars right first time – after all it took 35 years to hone the 911 to its current state of imperfect perfection. Let's hope the Boxster gets sorted a bit sooner than that."

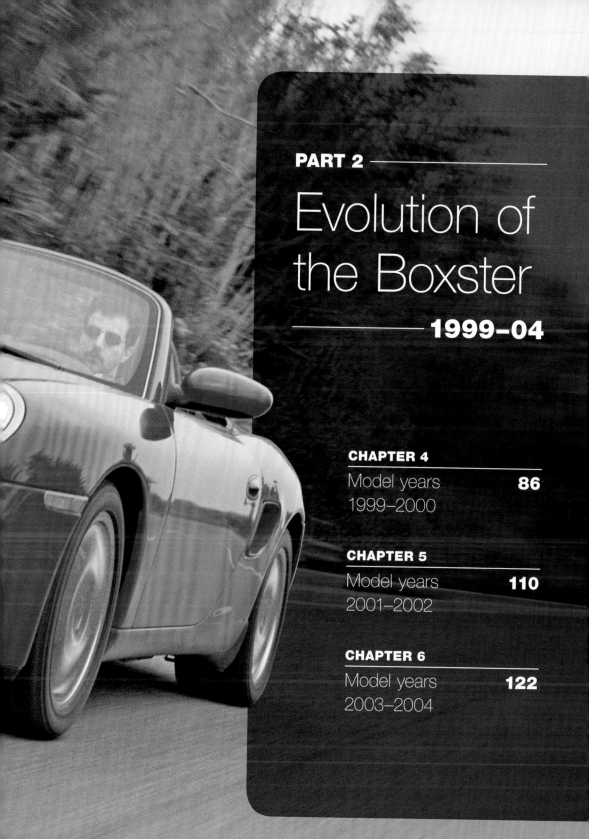

PART 2

Evolution of the Boxster

1999–04

CHAPTER 4

Model years 1999–2000

In its model year 1997 specification, the Boxster was an enormous success. It earned Porsche a large number of new customers; so many that, due to insufficient assembly line capacity next to the 911, Porsche could not meet the demand and had to have recourse to the independent Finnish Valmet Automotive company to help with the final assembly of the new model. Teething troubles were few. However, progress and legal requirements (mainly those regarding exhaust emissions) required punctual evolutions to keep the model both legal and competitive.

The Boxster's external shape and its interior appointments remained virtually unchanged from the model's introduction at the end of 1996 to the end of 2004, except for the very minor retouches that would come with the introduction of the 2003 models. Its chassis was so good that both the press and customers demanded more power, which came at no extra cost with the model year 2000 cars. Not only was the stroke of the 2.5-litre engine increased to bring its capacity up to 2.7 litres and the power from 201 to 217bhp (204 to 220PS) but simultaneously the Boxster family was complemented by the more expensive 3.2-litre Boxster S, featuring a six-speed gearbox and larger brakes to match the 249bhp (252PS) produced by the engine.

MODEL YEAR 1999

For 1999 the Boxster remained basically unchanged, but three important options were offered:

1 The PCM (Porsche Communication System) – a complete 'infotainment' system including radio, CD player, telephone and navigation system.

2 18in diameter wheels with the following specifications (RO = Wheel rim offset):
Front 7.5J 18 H2 RO 50 for 225/45 ZR 18 tyres.
The front track becomes 1,485mm.
Rear 9J 18 H2 RO 52 for 265/35 ZR 18 tyres.
The rear track becomes 1,504mm.

3 Litronic Xenon passing headlights in which the low beam H7 bulb and reflector are replaced with a poly-ellipsoid light unit containing a D2S gas-discharge lamp and carrying the control unit triggering the initial discharge with a tension of over 18,000 volts and keeping up the discharge with a 400 volt, 400Hz indirect current. The Litronic beam produces approximately twice the light compared with the standard beam, with 30 per cent less current consumption. To avoid glaring oncoming traffic under all conditions, the Litronic headlights come with high-pressure headlight washer jets and dynamic beam height control. The beam height control unit calculates the car's incidence angle from ride height sensors linked to the front and rear suspensions and operates step-by-step motors adjusting the position of the light reflectors accordingly. When the main beam is switched on, the motors raise the Litronic low beams to add light to the main beams.

▼ **Automatic headlight beam adjustment. (The automatic headlight adjustment is optional, but legally required if Xenon headlights (Litronic) are specified.)**

1 Control unit
2 Front axle angle sensor
3 Rear axle angle sensor
4 Step-by-step motor controlling the headlight angle
5 Headlight
6 Signals: wheel speed sensor, tension control

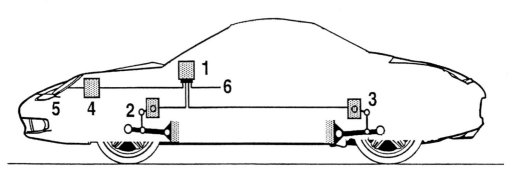

MODEL YEAR 2000

Once in full swing, the yearly production of the Boxster settled at around 30,000 units, equal to the production of the 996-series 911. Porsche however had not remained deaf to the mild but nevertheless frequent criticism, expressed by the press when the car was launched, of the comparative lack of torque in the 2,000 to 4,500rpm range. So, for the model year 2000 the capacity of the Boxster's engine was increased from 2.5 to 2.7 litres and a new variant, the 3.2-litre Boxster S, was launched.

BODY

Externally the basic Boxster, now with a 2.7-litre engine, was the same as its predecessor. The new 3.2-litre Boxster S was easily identified by the additional air intake in the front skirt to feed the third radiator fitted to Tiptronic-equipped models, by its twin exhaust tail pipes, by its standard 17in wheels and lower profile tyres (wheel and tyre sizes as the 17in option for the basic Boxster) and by its titanium-coloured front air intakes.

▼ The 3.2-litre Boxster S, introduced for the 2000 model year

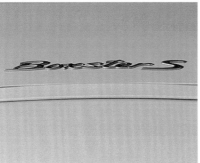

▲ A third front air intake is exclusive to the Boxster S. It feeds air to a third radiator only in cars equipped with Tiptronic S

◀ Boxster S script on rear boot lid

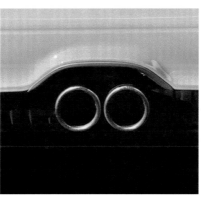

◀ Twin tail pipes were exclusive to the Boxster S

The Boxster S alone had a soft top with an additional cloth inner lining, reducing cabin noise levels. For both models, an effort was made to provide an impression of better quality, mainly by varnishing all the visible plastic components and by the use of more natural looking artificial leather, while the central section of the seats was trimmed in Alcantara and an 'aluminium look' was given to several fittings. More important than those cosmetic measures were the standard side airbags in the doors, the height adjustment extended to the passenger seat, the new and very elegant three-spoke steering wheel and the illuminated make-up mirrors. In the Boxster S the dashboard instruments were white with black digits; in the basic Boxster 2.7 they were black with white digits.

THE NEW M96/22 2.7-LITRE AND M96/21 3.2-LITRE ENGINES

▼ Power and torque curves of the Boxster 2.7-litre M96/22 engine. (Model years 2000–2002)

The two new engine variants for the Boxster range were introduced in September 1999. The engine capacity of the basic Boxster was increased to 2,687cc, obtained by using the 996-

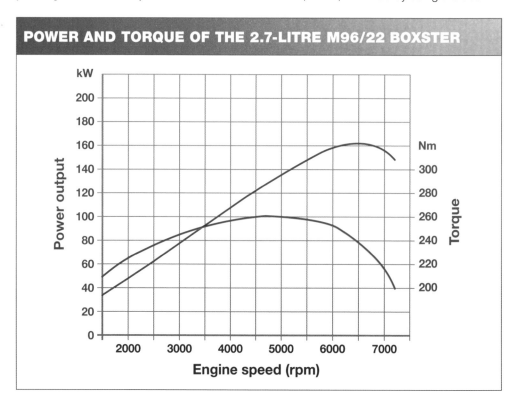

POWER AND TORQUE OF THE 2.7-LITRE M96/22 BOXSTER

series 911 crankshaft to increase
the stroke from 72 to 78mm. The
height of the pistons above the
gudgeon pin was reduced by
3mm to maintain the original
11.0:1 compression ratio. The
camshafts and their timing
were unchanged. The result
was a power increase to
217bhp (220PS) at 6,400rpm,
the torque now culminating at
192lb ft (260Nm) at 4,750rpm with a much
fatter and regular torque curve below 4,200rpm, due to
the addition of a resonance pipe, connecting the two plenum
chambers of the intake system, in which a vacuum-operated
resonance butterfly valve, governed by the DME was fitted.
Opening between 3,000rpm and 5,120rpm under loading and
closing 120rpm lower when decelerating (to avoid hunting), the
resonance valve makes use of the pulsations of the intake air

▲ Resonance intake
manifold of M96/21
and M96/22 engines,
showing the location of
the new resonance pipe
and butterfly valve

▼ Power and torque
curves of the Boxster S
3.2-litre M96/21 engine.
(Model years 2000–2002)

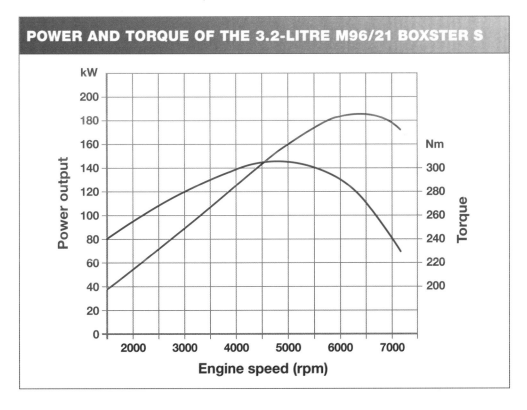

POWER AND TORQUE OF THE 3.2-LITRE M96/21 BOXSTER S

Power output (kW)

Torque (Nm)

Engine speed (rpm)

▲ The M96/22 2.7-litre and M96/21 3.2-litre engines had a revised intake system featuring an additional 'resonance' pipe connecting the two plenum chambers

between the two cylinder banks to improve the filling of the cylinders. Below and above this range, the valve remains closed.

For the M96/21 Boxster S engine, the same crankshaft was used as for the 2.7 engine, giving a stroke of 78mm, but the bore was increased to 93mm (as in the M96/01 engine of the 3.4-litre 996-series 911), resulting in a capacity of 3,179cc. The maximum power of 248bhp (252PS) was obtained at 6,250rpm, with the maximum torque of 225lb ft (305Nm) being available at 4,500rpm. The compression ratio was 11.0:1 and, as in the 2.7-litre engine, the pistons had an overall height of 53mm with 145mm long connecting rods. To match the important capacity increase, the valve sizes were increased from 33.3mm to 37.1mm on the intake and from 28.1mm to 31.5mm on the exhaust side, the port sizes being increased to match. The intake system with the added resonance valve and its functions were as in the 2.7-litre engine. For both engines the rev limit was now 7,200rpm.

The exhaust camshafts of the 3.2-litre engine were very similar to the 2.7-litre's, but the intake camshafts were new, increasing the valve opening duration from 210° to 226° (at 1mm valve lift). This resulted in the following timing:

'Early' diagram: Intake   opens 11° before TDC
                                  closes 35° after BDC

'Late' diagram: Intake   opens 14° after TDC
                                  closes 60° after BDC

                        Exhaust   opens 39° before BDC
                                  closes 6° before TDC

▼ Ghosted view of
the 2000 Boxster

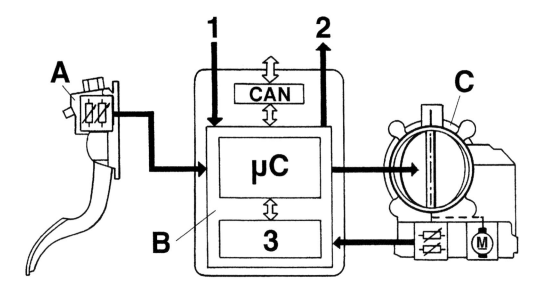

▲ Principle drawing
of the 'drive-by-wire'
throttle-valve control
system.
A Accelerator pedal
B Motronic engine
   management unit
   (DME)
C Throttle valve
   control unit with
   step-by-step
   electric motor
1 Messages to the
   Motronic unit
2 Outgoing messages
   to various functions
3 Supervising module

Both new engines were managed by a higher performance Bosch 7.2 Motronic DME, which, in addition to all the functions of the 5.2.2 Motronic, integrated two important new attributes:

■ An electronically monitored throttle valve operated by a step-by-step electric motor ('drive by wire')
■ The 'torque-oriented function'

The 'torque-oriented function' adjusts the throttle valve opening and the ignition timing in such a way that whatever the conditions in which the engine operates and whatever the power absorbed by the ancillaries, such as the generator or air-conditioning compressor, the torque available at the flywheel for any given position of the accelerator pedal is always the same. The DME coordinates the automatic torque reduction required by the Porsche Stability Management (PSM) and by the Tiptronic transmission to further smoothen the up- and downshifts and to prevent over-revving. In addition, the DME also integrates the engine's 700rpm idle speed control. The accelerator pedal is connected by a cable to a potentiometer located under the dash

structure. The potentiometer
signals the torque required to the
DME, which integrates it together
with torque requirements from
other sources and from factors
affecting the engine efficiency (air,
oil, water temperatures for example).
The DME then energises the throttle valve motor to
open the throttle valve to the exact angle corresponding to the
required torque, irrespective of the other consumers, but with a
priority given to safety systems such as Traction Control (TC), or
Porsche Stability Management (PSM), if fitted.

For the German and USA markets, the Boxster and the
Boxster S were fitted with a new trimetal catalyst (palladium
was added to rhodium and platinum as catalytic agents) and an
electric secondary air pump to qualify as an LEV (Low Emission
Vehicle) in America and to meet the even stricter D4 German
emission norms. For the USA a quick heating start catalyst was
bolted directly to the modified exhaust manifold.

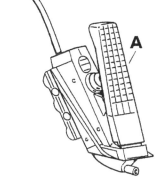

◀ 'Drive-by-wire' actuator.
A Accelerator pedal
B Pedal position
   transmitter

TRANSMISSION

The capacity increase of the basic Boxster engine from 2.5 to 2.7 litres for the 2000 model year required modifications to its gear ratios while a new six-speed manual gearbox was developed for the 3.2-litre Boxster S.

The type G86/01 five-speed manual gearbox differs from the G86/00 box (used in the 2.5-litre Boxster) only by its internal and final drive ratios. The individual gear pairs are shown below.

In the A86/01 Tiptronic S transmission, only the final drive ratio was changed, from 4.21:1 to 4.02:1

The Boxster S, from the beginning of its production, came with a six-speed manual gearbox, a development of the five-speed box of the basic Boxster. Reverse gear is selected in a fourth plane of the shift pattern, far left and forward from the neutral position. The ratios are shown opposite.

The optional Tiptronic transmission of the Boxster S was the same as for the basic Boxster 2.5-litre and 2.7-litre, except for the final drive ratio of 3.73:1. The torque converter diameter

G86/01 MANUAL GEARBOX GEAR RATIOS

Gear	Gear teeth pairing	Output: input ratio	mph at 1,000rpm
1st	10/35	3.500	5.77
2nd	17/36	2.118	9.60
3rd	28/40	1.429	14.15
4th	33/36	1.091	18.50
5th	37/31	0.838	24.00
Reverse		3.440	
Final drive		3.56	

is 254mm (10in) and the stall speed is 2,400rpm. The weight of the complete gearbox and differential unit is 112.5kg and adds 50kg to the complete car, compared to the manual six-speed gearbox unit.

For 2000, all Tiptronic-equipped Boxsters benefited from a convenient manual override feature, which allowed the driver

BOXSTER S 6 SPEED MANUAL GEARBOX

Gear	Gear teeth pairing	Output: input ratio	mph at 1,000rpm
1st	11/42	3.82	5.50
2nd	20/44	2.20	9.55
3rd	31/47	1.52	13.82
4th	37/45	1.22	17.12
5th	41/42	1.02	20.60
6th	44/37	0.84	25.00
Reverse		3.55	
Final drive		3.44	

▲ The workplace of a Boxster S with the full PCM equipment

to make gear changes using the steering wheel switches even when driving in the automatic mode. The gear selected in this way remains in operation for about eight seconds before the system returns to the automatic mode, except if the car is on the overrun or when it is cornering with a lateral acceleration exceeding 0.5g, or is on a steep down slope.

STANDARD SUSPENSION

	Boxster		Boxster S	
	front	rear	front	rear
Spring rate at wheel (N/mm)	24	27	24	30
Dampers	two-tubes, gas filled		two-tubes, gas filled	
Frequency, no load (Hz)	1.55	1.51	1.54	1.55
Tubular anti-roll bar,	23.1	18.5	23.6	19.0
dia x thickness (mm)	x3.4	x2.5	x3.5	x2.7

SPORT SUSPENSION

	Boxster		Boxster S	
	front	rear	front	rear
Spring rate at wheel (N/mm)	30	35.5	30	37
Dampers	two-tubes, gas filled		two-tubes, gas filled	
Frequency, no load (Hz)	1.7	1.7	1.7	1.7
Tubular anti-roll bar,	23.6	19.6	24.0	19.6
dia x thickness (mm)	x3.5	x2.6	x3.8	x2.6

▶ 17in wheels are standard on the Boxster S which inherits the large brakes of the 911 with red finished monobloc callipers

SUSPENSION MODIFICATIONS

Taking into account the higher power of the Boxster S and its optional high-performance tyres, the new model received reinforced rear wheel carriers and wheel bearings, with slightly longer track arms for reduced toe-in variations. The corresponding track rods were pivoted on harder rubber bushes for better straight-line stability. In addition to stiffer anti-roll bars, stiffer rear springs and appropriately tuned dampers took care of the more sporting performance of the Boxster S. The basic Boxster also received the harder rear track rod bushes.

BRAKES

While the brakes of the basic Boxster remained unchanged, the Boxster S inherited the brakes of the 911 Carrera. As in the original Boxster, aluminium 'monobloc' four-piston callipers are used front and rear. But the discs of the Boxster S are larger, thicker and perforated. The 28mm thick front discs with curved internal cooling channels have a diameter of 318mm (Boxster 298 x 24mm), while the 24mm rear discs have grown to 298mm (Boxster 282 x 20mm) and still include the cable-operated two leading-shoe parking brake. A pressure limiter is incorporated in the rear braking circuit.

PRESS COMMENTS

The 2000 model

Generally speaking, the press paid much more attention to the Boxster S than to the base Boxster, now with an uprated engine. Despite the welcome increase in power and torque, in a comparison test by the German *Auto Motor und Sport* (22 October 1999) in which a Boxster 2.7 was compared to the 225PS

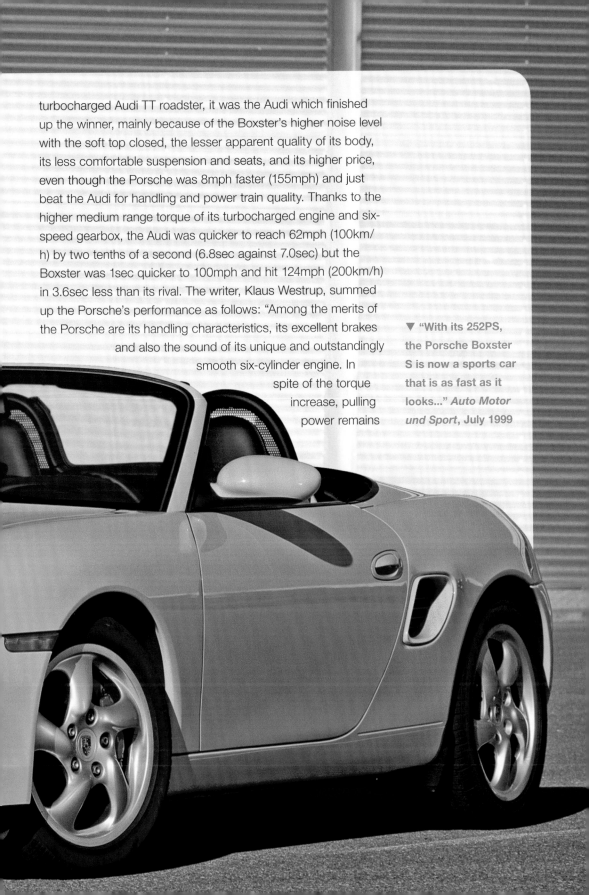

turbocharged Audi TT roadster, it was the Audi which finished
up the winner, mainly because of the Boxster's higher noise level
with the soft top closed, the lesser apparent quality of its body,
its less comfortable suspension and seats, and its higher price,
even though the Porsche was 8mph faster (155mph) and just
beat the Audi for handling and power train quality. Thanks to the
higher medium range torque of its turbocharged engine and six-
speed gearbox, the Audi was quicker to reach 62mph (100km/
h) by two tenths of a second (6.8sec against 7.0sec) but the
Boxster was 1sec quicker to 100mph and hit 124mph (200km/h)
in 3.6sec less than its rival. The writer, Klaus Westrup, summed
up the Porsche's performance as follows: "Among the merits of
the Porsche are its handling characteristics, its excellent brakes
and also the sound of its unique and outstandingly
smooth six-cylinder engine. In
spite of the torque
increase, pulling
power remains

▼ "With its 252PS,
the Porsche Boxster
S is now a sports car
that is as fast as it
looks..." *Auto Motor
und Sport*, July 1999

rather modest. As far as suspension comfort and interior noise are concerned, the Porsche is beaten by its challenger, and this is also the case in the impression of its visible quality."

Writing about the Boxster S, *Auto Motor und Sport* (14 July 1999) writer Wolfgang König was much kinder than his colleague starting his test report with: "At last the Boxster gets what it had always deserved: more power. With its 252PS [248bhp], the Porsche Boxster S is now a sports car that is as fast as it looks... The result meets the wishes of many Boxster drivers. 252PS ensures power reserves one expects from a Porsche, but even more welcome is the jump in torque from 245Nm (181lb ft) to 305Nm (225lb ft), available at 4,500rpm. And Porsche has also made a concession to the joy provided by a keenly revving engine and has raised the red line from 6,700 to 7,200rpm." Concerning handling and comfort, the tester proceeds: "As before, a 'sport' running gear is an option in which the ride height is lowered by 10mm. But the test car had the standard set-up, uprated by the optional 18inch wheels and traction control, providing an exemplary compromise between comfort

▼ All Porsche press cars carry a PR registration number, the S standing for Stuttgart

and sportivity ... Exemplary are also the traction and the straight-line stability, but what above all mirrors the art with which the suspension is set up, is the ride comfort. Without spoiling the intimate contact with the road surface, Porsche has achieved real comfort without having recourse to sporting stiffnesses." Strange how much the subjective judgements of different testers writing for the same magazine can be at variance!

In a further twin test by *Auto Motor und Sport* (11 August 1999) involving a Boxster S and a 3-litre BMW M Roadster, the Porsche finishes up a clear winner, even though the much more powerful 317bhp (321PS) but similarly priced BMW easily leaves the Porsche behind with an advantage of nearly two seconds (12.3sec against 14.2sec) at 100mph and 3.4sec at 124mph. Tester Götz Leyrer writes: "The Porsche has an even more neutral handling (than the BMW) and is easier to control when forced into a powerslide." He concludes his article, writing: "[The BMW] is a fascinating toy, mostly desirable for its immense power. But the perfect work of art in this class is the Porsche Boxster." And he sums it up: "The new Porsche convinces by

Boxster S with
optional hardtop

its overall balance. In the S-version the engine has gained a lot of pulling power, but its smoothness has remained untouched. Its handling and its brakes set benchmarks. It also owes its victory to the all-round qualities of its body and the harmonious set-up of its suspension."

This twin test was duplicated by *Autocar* (14 July 1999). "In a straight line, the BMW pulverises its (Boxster S) opponent ... The powerful BMW's advantage disappears on twisty roads where it pays heavily for its ageing underpinnings ... The BMW throws into sharp focus just how good the Boxster's chassis is. On typical A or B roads, the Porsche is not only the quicker of the two, but also the most entertaining ... In the end, so convincing is the Boxster's victory that the contest feels almost like a mismatch."

In its test of the entry level Boxster 2.7, *Autocar* (10 November 1999) disagreed with *Auto Motor und Sport* about the pulling power of the 2.7-litre Boxster and wrote: "Although the 0–60mph time has improved by just a fraction (6.4sec versus 6.5sec), the dash to 100mph is a much more significant yardstick and shows where the real differences lie between the old and the new car. The 2.7 hits the ton in 15.5sec, some 2.5 seconds quicker than

the 2.5-litre car. The 2.7 immediately feels quicker throughout the rev range, and this is born out by the in-gear acceleration figures. Pulling from 20mph in 4th or 5th gear, the 2.7 is consistently a second quicker over each of the 20mph increments up to 100mph, after which the gap grows wider still. Between 50mph and 70mph it is nearly two seconds quicker ... The hike in performance has only marginally dented fuel economy. Driven sensibly, the 2.7 can still return 30mpg." Concerning handling and comfort the testers are hardly in favour of options. "The Boxster remains a sublime 'compagnon' on the road. Porsche has wisely left the chassis well alone. The test car's optional 17in wheels and ultra-low profile rubber look great, but do nothing for the low speed ride quality ... Body roll is minimal, yet the suspension is supple enough over fast undulations to keep the car totally stable, with all four wheels in contact with the tarmac. This coupled with steering that is well weighted and delightfully responsive, and brakes that are as powerful as they come, makes the Boxster a joy to drive over deserted roads." And the article concludes with: "Indeed the entry level Boxster is so far improved that it makes us

wonder about the wisdom of spending another £8,000 on the only slightly more sensational S model."

This is also the opinion of Mike Duff, writing for *Car* (December 1999), whose test report is titled "Why pay more for S?" He writes: "The Boxster is still as fun to drive slowly as it always was. It's a generic Porsche thing: the super directness of the tactile, drivey bits and the challenge of slotting everything together neatly. The car is as focused as ever, a slack-free zone. And of course fun to drive fast as well. Okay, the S has arrived to provide the hardcore thrills. But in a slightly more laid-back way, the ordinary Boxster is just as good."

In *Car & Driver* (September 1999) Peter Robinson writes in his Boxster S preview: "Behind the wheel, the extra power (compared to the Boxster 2.7) is immediately apparent ... The 3.2 engine still loves to rev, but by increasing mid-range power and raising the red line so significantly, the S feels far stronger and responsive just about everywhere than the base Boxster ... The problem now facing the marketing folks is to justify the Carrera cabriolet when the Boxster is almost as quick, is more fun to drive and costs a lot less."

▼ **"With the S, Porsche has at last unleashed the Boxster's true potential..."** *What Car?*, **November 1999**

The subtitle to the *Car & Driver* full test of the Boxster S says "A sports car to get sappy over – no ifs, and very few buts". In the last phrases of the test report, the speedometer dial is criticised for being too small and for "calling off speed in exceptionally wide, 25mph increments ... being worthless for gauging the speed ... [and] shows 3 to 4mph high at freeway speeds, an annoying error. That's a but... .

"The soft top's plastic back window is indisputably a but. Probably not a killer, though most assuredly an irritant one." The article nevertheless concludes with: "Porsche could have done better here, but we're going to stay on top of these concerns by driving S-model Boxsters every chance we get."

"At last the Boxster gets the power to exploit its chassis", writes the British *What Car?* (November 1999) which concludes its test report: "With the S, Porsche has at last unleashed the Boxster's true potential, and with it has come a 10 month waiting list. In fact the Boxster S is so good it makes the £30,000 dearer 911 cabriolet seem almost redundant, and there's no higher praise than that."

CHAPTER 5

Model years 2001–2002

Following the previous year's revisions, and the introduction of the new, more powerful 2.7-litre and 3.2-litre 'S' engines, the Boxster received higher praise than ever. The Boxster S drew much of the attention, often compared with the contemporary 911 in terms of performance and driver appeal. The next two years would see little change in the Boxster's appearance, but minor improvements in the cockpit and to the engine, together with the introduction of the optional Porsche Stability Management (PSM) system, ensured that the cars remained competitive in the marketplace.

MODEL YEAR 2001 ———————————————

BODY

The Boxster 2.7 now came with the soft-top cloth inner lining, which previously had been a feature unique to the Boxster S. Both models also got thicker front and rear luggage boot mats. The levers operating the front and rear luggage boots by cables were replaced with switches operating the locks electrically. For safety reasons, the switches must be pulled up to open the boots. Next to them, on the driver's door sill, are the push buttons for the optional triple seat and mirror memory. The memory and the boot locks could now also be operated by remote control with the ignition key, while electro-chrome automatic anti-glare cockpit and external mirrors were a new option. Also new was an LED (light-emitting diode) 'orientation light' located above the interior rear-view mirror, which could be used safely at night without causing distraction.

The dashboard instruments were revised and were now operated by just two CAN-Bus (multiplex) lines, one for the

These two shots of a
Boxster 2.7 show the
car equipped with the
optional wind deflectors

▲ The driver's door
sill showing the front
and rear boot release
switches and the
triple seat and mirror
memory buttons

power train and one for the car's interior. The digital speed
display is part of the analogue speedometer, together with
the Tempomat (speed control) warning lamp, while the
distance and trip recorders are part of the computer displays
in the rev-counter dial which, when starting the engine,
automatically display the engine oil level and the waiting time
for a correct reading of the gauge. The digital clock is included
in the right-hand dial together with the oil pressure and water
temperature gauges.

ENGINE

The existing hardware of both engines was carried over to
2001, except for the camshaft drives in which the duplex primary
roller chain (between the crankshaft and the intermediate shaft)
was replaced by a more silent toothed chain. This called for the
use of a new crankshaft and intermediate shaft, which were in
one piece with the new toothed wheels, and of a new primary
chain tensioner.

The software was modified to meet the requirements of the
new EOBD (Euro On Board Diagnostics) system demanded by

the Euro 3 emission regulations which also involved the use of a new tri-metal catalyst, already required by the 2000 regulations for cars sold in Germany and the USA. The EOBD requirements were met by adding a second oxygen (Lambda) sensor downstream of the catalyst to check the quality of the exhaust gases expelled into the atmosphere. During operation, a permanent warning light is activated on the instrument panel if exhaust gas quality does not meet the legal requirements. If the problem poses a risk of damaging the catalyst, the warning light flashes intermittently. The origin of the malfunction can then be diagnosed with the equipment available in all Porsche dealerships.

RUNNING GEAR, STEERING AND DRIVING AIDS

An important option, the Porsche Stability Management, became available on 2001 model year Boxster and Boxster S models. Generally better known as ESP (Electronic Stability Programme), the system was initially introduced as standard in the 2000 model year 911 Carrera 4.

▼ PSM (stability management) system.
1 PSM control unit with relay
2 Hydraulic unit
3 Polar rotation sensor
4 Wheel rpm sensor
5 Pre-charge pump
6 Pressure sensor
7 'PSM off' switch
8 Stop light switch
9 Warning lights
10 Info-lamp
11 Stop lights
12 Steering angle sensor
13 Hand brake warning light switch
14 DME unit

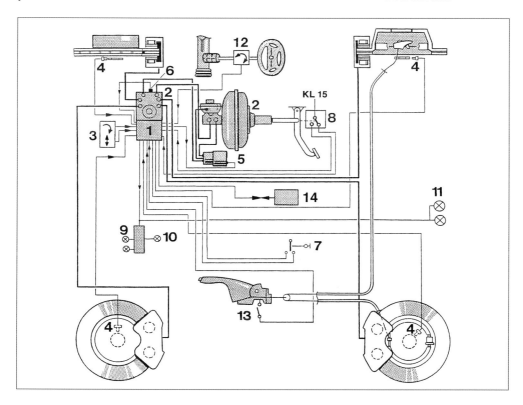

The system amalgamates the TC (Traction Control), the MSR (Motor Schleppmoment-Regelung or engine brake regulation) and an evolution of the ABD (Automatic Brake Differential). The MSR performs an opposite function to the TC and requires a short explanation. On a very slippery surface and in a low gear, when the accelerator pedal is lifted, the engine braking can be too strong for the grip available, causing the wheels to slide. This is sensed by the slower rotating speed of the driven wheels compared to the non-driven wheels and is communicated by the ABS wheel sensors to the PSM control unit, which instantly re-opens the throttle very slightly to re-establish the grip of the driving wheels.

The PSM is not compatible with a limited-slip differential. Its traction control function, which includes stopping a spinning wheel by promptly operating the appropriate brake and transferring the excess torque to the opposite wheel, requires a free-operating differential. In the PSM the function of the electronically-controlled hydraulic unit is extended to controlling all four brakes individually, if required, to keep the understeering

▼ PSM was an important option, ensuring stability and grip, particularly in slippery conditions

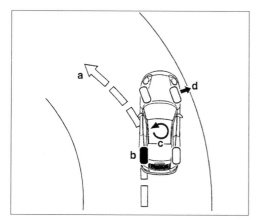 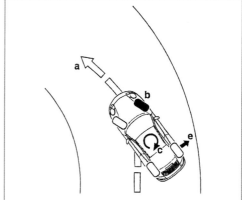

or oversteering car on the line chosen by the driver. Which brake is applied and when is decided essentially by three different sorts of sensor:

- The four ABS wheel sensors providing real time information about the rotating speed of each individual wheel (from this data the car's speed, its acceleration or deceleration, as well as wheel spin or trail, are calculated by the PSM control unit);
- The sensor for the car's polar rotating speed and lateral acceleration, located in the car's central console, as near as possible to the centre of gravity; and
- The sensor for the steering wheel angle.

The data obtained from these sensors is compared by the PSM unit with the memorised data corresponding to normal progress. In the case of a discrepancy, the PSM intervenes automatically to stabilise the car.

If a discrepancy is registered when the car is driven in a straight line, the PSM operates either as an ABS, individually controlling any braked wheel tending to lock, or as a traction control, combining the functions of the ABD (Automatic Brake Differential) and ASR (Automatic Spin Control). The system may also reduce engine torque by retarding the ignition and, if necessary, reducing the throttle opening.

When the car is cornering, the PSM, which is continuously informed of the speed at which the wheels rotate, of the lateral acceleration, of the car's polar rotational speed and of the steering wheel angle, compares this data with that memorised

▲ Porsche Stability Management (PSM). The left-hand drawing shows an understeering car in a left curve. To bring it back on the desired course shown by the arrow (a), the left rear wheel is braked, creating a torque around the car's centre of gravity (c), helping the driver to bring the car back on course. The right-hand drawing shows an oversteering car in a similar curve. In that case, the right hand front wheel brake is activated to create the stabilising torque around the centre of gravity for the same speed and steering angle under normal cornering conditions. Any anomaly in the car's behaviour, such as wheel spin or oversteer and understeer is thus immediately detected and corrected by automatically operating the brake controlling the appropriate wheel. Here are some examples:

The car makes a left turn and understeers excessively. By operating the left rear brake, the PSM creates a torque around the car's centre of gravity, helping the car to turn into the bend. The braking action ceases as soon as the correct parameters have been restored.

The car makes a left turn and oversteers excessively. In this case, the right front brake is operated to bring the rear of the car back on the correct line.

If selective operation of the brakes is insufficient to stabilise the car, the PSM reduces the engine torque, first by retarding the ignition and then by reducing the throttle opening.

How far the car is allowed to get out of shape is a matter of tuning the system and is left to the manufacturer.

Many sports car drivers like to control their car as much as possible themselves and often like to deliberately create an oversteering attitude. Porsche has reacted to their request and has tuned the PSM so as to give those drivers a fair margin to exercise their skills before the electronics intervene. When it does, a warning light flashes on the car's instrument panel. The PSM can be switched off by pushing a button on the dash panel, but for safety reasons it is instantly reactivated as soon as the driver touches the brake pedal in a situation where the preset margin for PSM intervention has been exceeded.

In the case of any malfunction, the PSM is automatically switched off and warning lights are activated on the dash panel, indicating which of the functions is faulty. The fault is automatically memorised and its origin can be diagnosed and corrected with the appropriate equipment at Porsche dealerships.

As usual with switchable safety systems, if the PSM has been switched off, it is reactivated every time the ignition is switched on.

MODEL YEAR 2002

BODY

The only changes for the 2002 model year were the introduction of an even more sophisticated anti-theft system and an optional new and faster-calculating navigation system.

ENGINE

While the two types of engine remained basically unchanged, the fuel and exhaust systems benefited from developments made by the suppliers.

In 2002-on models, the fuel pressure is controlled by a pressure-limiting valve integrated, together with the fuel filter, in the tank to which any excess fuel is directly returned. This avoids the long loop of the excess fuel through the injection ramps and back to the tank where it warms the tank's content, reducing the fuel's density. The underfloor fuel filter is deleted.

Other modifications were a switch to smaller, lighter and less heat-sensitive type four-hole injectors; to smaller and lighter

Lambda sensors, which become operative at lower temperatures than before; to a new type of hot-film air mass sensor, less sensitive to dirt and water drops; and to new four-electrode spark plugs in which the spark runs along the ceramic isolator. These plugs have a useful life of 50,000 miles.

RUNNING GEAR, STEERING AND DRIVING AIDS

A new Bosch 5.7 PSM unit was introduced, differing from the preceding unit by having more 'linear' solenoid-operated valves. Instead of having only an 'open' and 'closed' position, the new valves open and close progressively. The resultant smoother selective automatic operation of the brakes in the PSM and ABS functions helps maintain grip on very slippery surfaces. The new installation also includes even more sensitive wheel rotation speed sensors, also sensing the direction of rotation.

A further minor modification was the stiffer and more reliable location of the front suspension subframe to the main body structure by four instead of two bolts. This has no effect on the other suspension components or the handling, but is an easy means of 'dating' a car.

Externally both the 2.7 and 3.2 models remain unchanged for 2002, except for a more sophisticated anti-theft system and a higher performance optional navigation system

CHAPTER 6

Model years 2003–2004

In September 2002, the Boxster and Boxster S models were given a minor face lift as well as an 8bhp (8PS) power increase. After their introduction, production of the Boxster and Boxster S continued unchanged until the arrival of the 987 model range.

BODY

The most obvious modifications were the restyled front and rear skirts, both with a more pronounced lower lip and, at the rear, new stylish air exits from under the car. The air intakes on the body sides were slightly lengthened and the retractable rear spoiler was restyled without affecting its efficiency. The standard Boxster retained the same 16in wheels as before, but the 17in wheels of the Boxster S were a new design and five per cent lighter than previously. They were available as an option for the basic Boxster and even 18in wheels, saving a total of 10.8kg compared with the previous model, were available for both lines.

Both the Boxster and Boxster S received a further improved hood. The cloth head lining had been common to both models since the model year 2001, but for the 2003 models the hood structure was modified with an added arch to accept an electrically-heated 3.15mm thick safety glass rear window,

replacing the fragile soft vinyl window. The sizes of the hood box and of the capacity of the rear boot were unchanged.

A large glovebox was now provided under the airbag in front of the passenger seat and a cup holder for two cups or bottles slid from between the central air outlet and the new, second-generation PCM display screen in the central part of the dash structure.

The Boxster and Boxster S have not escaped the tendency of cars to put on some weight as the years pass. Inevitably the more comprehensive equipment required partly by laws, partly by the market, together with the reinforcement of various components accompanying power increases, have progressively increased the weight of the Boxster since its introduction. From 1,250kg without extras in 1997, the weight of the basic Boxster increased to 1,275kg in 2003 and the same increase of 25kg raised the weight of the Boxster S to 1,320kg in its first four years of production, according to Porsche's official figures. The main reason for the 45kg difference between the Boxster and Boxster S is the latter's heavier brakes and air

▼ The rear aerofoil was redesigned for better integration when retracted

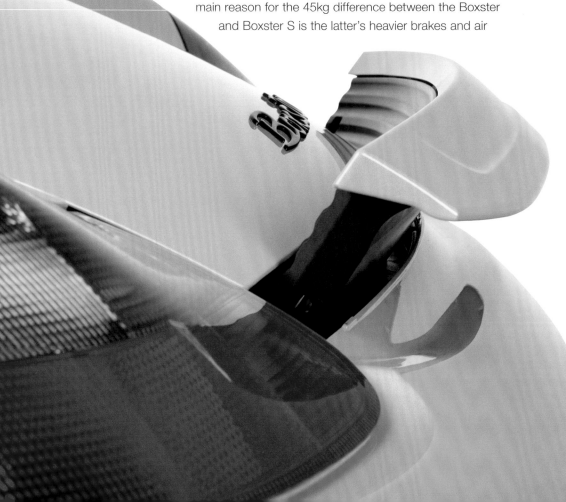

conditioning, which is standard in the 'S' but is an option in the base model and is consequently not included in the standard car's weight. The weights quoted in independent road tests are invariably higher than Porsche's figures, because test cars usually come with numerous optional extras.

▲ The lateral air intakes were slightly reshaped for 2003

ENGINES

Both the Boxster and Boxster S engines underwent important modifications for 2003. The most important change was to the Variocam system in which the intake camshaft angle was now varied by a progressive hydraulic vane-type variator. To control the new Variocam, a Bosch Motronic 7.8 replaced the Motronic 7.2. These changes resulted in a two per cent improvement in fuel consumption, while both engines benefited from a power increase of 8bhp.

A minor contribution to the power increase came from the cylinder blocks: the lower end of the cylinders were partly cut out so as to allow an easier air circulation inside the crankcase, thereby reducing the pumping losses caused by the alternating movements of the pistons.

2003 ENGINE PERFORMANCE DATA

	M 96/23 (Boxster)	M 96/24 (Boxster S)
Max power at rpm	225bhp (228PS) at 6,300rpm	256bhp (260PS) at 6,200rpm
Max torque at rpm	192lb ft (260Nm) at 4,700rpm	229lb ft (310Nm) at 4,600rpm

THE NEW VARIOCAM AND CAMSHAFT DRIVE

The 2003 model Boxster's M96/23 and Boxster S's M96/24 engines differed from their predecessors mainly by the camshaft drive and the replacement of the chain-tensioner type intake camshaft angle variator with a vane-type variator, which adjusts the timing continuously over an angle of 40° measured on the crankshaft, as is the case in the 911's M96/03 engine since the 2002 model. This involved a change of the camshaft drive with both camshafts of either engine side being now driven from the intermediate shaft by a single chain. The chain tensioners were modified accordingly.

The variator consists of a cylindrical stator, which is toothed at its periphery and driven by the timing chain, and contains a rotor screwed to the camshaft. Inside the stator five peripheral chambers are provided into which the five radial vanes of the rotor penetrate. Pressurised oil is ducted from the centre of the rotor to either side of the vanes and fills the chambers on one or other side of the vanes. The oil pressure rotates the rotor (and the camshaft) a maximum of 20° in either direction, modifying the valve timing over a range of 40°. The timing variations are

◄ Cutaway view of the 2003 Boxster S M96/24 engine

▼ Crankcase of the M96/23 and M96/24 engines. The arrow shows the new recesses in the cylinder bore walls facilitating the movement of the air contained in the crankcase to reduce the pressure build-up under the pistons when they move down

decided, as before, by the DME operating a solenoid controlling a four-way valve fed by the engine's lubrication system and controlling the flow of oil to and from the Variocam unit. By interrupting the flow to and from the Variocam unit, the four-way control valve can keep the rotor in any position between the two extremes, any leakage being instantly corrected by appropriate movements of the control valve. When the engine is stopped, a pin contained in the stator is pushed by a spring into a recess of the stator, holding the camshaft in the 'late timing' position. This avoids any knock before the oil pressure builds up sufficiently to push the pin back to release the rotor.

To activate the new Variocam the 7.2 Motronic DME (engine management), which had replaced the Motronic 5.2.2 in the 2000 models, had to be exchanged again

▶ Ghosted view of
2003 Boxster S

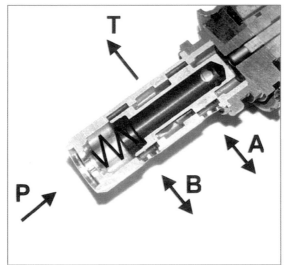

◀ Solenoid-operated four-way valve controlling the camshaft angle variator. Oil pressure (P) is applied to the bottom of the valve, controlled by a solenoid. According to whether the pressurised oil exits through A or B, the vanes in the cam angle variator rotate the camshaft in one or the other direction. By closing both exits the camshaft can be held in any intermediate position. Excess oil then flows back into the crankcase. (Arrow T)

► Intake camshaft
drive and Variocam
control in the M96/23
and 24 engines.

1 Crankshaft revolution
   sensor
2 Hall sensor
3 Real time camshaft
   angle
4 Camshaft adjustment
5 Required camshaft
   angle
6 4-way proportional
   valve
7 Cam angle variator
8 DME

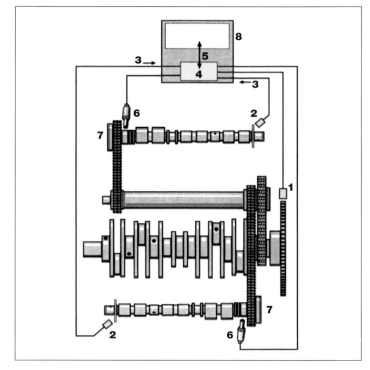

▼ The new 'Variocam'
of the M96/23 and 24
engine simplifies the
chain drive of
the camshafts

for the 7.8 Motronic required for the infinitely variable operation
of the intake camshaft timing, which is the main contributor to
the two per cent reduction in overall fuel consumption, to the
increase in the power and to the fatter torque curve available in
both the Boxster and Boxster S engines. The exhaust system has
also come in for further tuning, mainly to obtain a more musical
'sporting' sound.

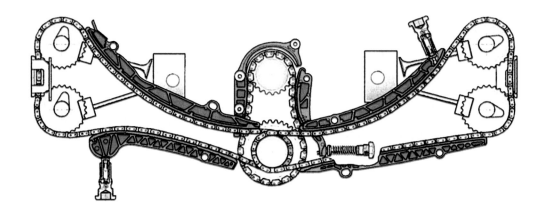

The new Variocam entailed several modifications to the cam box and cylinder head, but the valve sizes and their included angle were unchanged. The camshafts were also new because of the new timing variator, but the cams and valve opening duration were unchanged. New timings (at 1mm lift) are as follows:

2.7-litre M96/23 engine:

'Early' diagram: Intake   opens 21° before TDC
                           closes 9° after BDC

'Late' diagram: Intake   opens 19° after TDC
                           closes 49° after BDC

                     Exhaust   opens 39° before BDC
                           closes 8° before TDC

3.2-litre M96/24 engine:

'Early' diagram: Intake   opens 26° before TDC
                           closes 20° after BDC

'Late' diagram: Intake   opens 14° after TDC
                           closes 60° after BDC

                     Exhaust   opens 39° before BDC
                           closes 6° before TDC

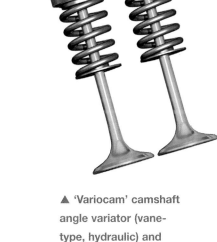

▲ 'Variocam' camshaft angle variator (vane-type, hydraulic) and intake valves

RUNNING GEAR, STEERING AND DRIVING AIDS

The additional horsepower developed by both the 2.7-litre and 3.2-litre engines did not require any significant change to the suspension, brakes or steering. Only the dampers were slightly recalibrated. The new cast-aluminium 17in ten-spoke and 18in five-spoke wheels were, however, lighter than before. A total of 2kg (5.6%) was saved on the former and as much as 10.8kg (22.1%) on the 18in wheels, a saving all the more significant since unsprung weight is directly related to handling and comfort.

The 2003 model

Autocar's verdict following the road test of the 2003 model Boxster 2.7 (23 October 2002) sums it up: "Hardly surprising really. Before this minor round of revisions, the Boxster was comfortably the most complete sports car for the money, and now Porsche has tipped a little extra of everything into the pot – in particular performance, style and practicality – the company

has moved the roadster even further out of its rivals' range. The success is thoroughly deserved, because the Boxer is a uniquely rounded package from a company whose image has been crafted through uncompromising road and race cars. It offers sufficient comfort and practicality for the cruiser, thrills enough for the enthusiast, and the dependability and reassurance demanded by the mainstream buyer. Not everyone will buy into the image, but on ability alone it's the most complete roadster you can currently buy."

While *Autocar* ranks the 2003 model Boxster 2.7 at the top of its class with nine stars out of a possible ten (the BMW Z4 gets only seven, the Mercedes SLK 3.2 six), the BMW Z4 3.0 emerges as the winner of an *Auto Motor und Sport* (16 April 2003) back-to-back comparison test with the €2,358 [£1,627 approx.] more expensive Boxster 2.7. The reasons are not technical excellence, performance, handling, comfort or build quality. The Boxster loses mainly because of its higher price, more spartan equipment and the higher cost of optional equipment.

▼ The 2003 Boxster (right) and Boxster S with restyled front and rear skirts

▲ For 2003, the layout of the instruments was revised. The digital speedometer is now contained in the analogue speedometer dial. White instruments denote a Boxster S. The three-spoke airbag steering wheel was introduced on 2000 models

In its 7 August 2002 issue, *Auto Motor und Sport* nevertheless gives the face-lifted Boxster S its top five-star rating commenting: "Porsche's small step development policy includes technical developments as well as a face lift. As in the latest 911 models, the Boxster's engine has benefited from now continuously variable intake camshaft timing. The result is 2% less overall fuel consumption in the European test cycle, together with an extra 8PS ... Instead of reaching 100km/h (62mph) in 6.1 seconds, only 5.7 seconds are now needed, and by the time 200km/h (124mph) are reached (in 13.5sec) 1.9 seconds have been saved ... and maximum speed is up from 260 to 264km/h (164mph)." The tester concludes: "The Boxster S meets in exemplary manner the requirements traditionally expected from the Zuffenhausen company. It is a full-blood sports car, perfectly adapted to everyday use."

"If it ain't broke, don't fix it." With this old American aphorism, Joe Rusz, *Road & Track*'s Porsche specialist, started his first driving impressions of the 2003 model Boxsters. "A day of driving in the Italian countryside south of Rome reaffirmed what we have known for six years: the Boxster delivers even more bang

◀ Customers had to wait until 2003 for a glovebox

per buck (or euphoria per Euro) than any other Porsche model ... Although the overall performance of the 2003 models is not noticeably different, the low speed driveability is definitely improved. And thanks to retuning the intake and exhaust systems, both Boxsters now make a lovely low-speed growl ... Prices remain unchanged, proof that Porsche understands another American aphorism: Don't mess with success."

▼ From 2003, the Boxster was fitted with a heated glass rear window

CHAPTER 7

Model year 2005

Since its introduction, the Boxster has undergone various revisions, principally on the mechanical side, which answered early criticisms of the car's lack of power and brought further steady improvements in performance and refinement to the point where the overall package was considered almost perfect. However, in the meantime some serious competitors had come up, such as the BMW Z4 and the Mercedes-Benz 350SLK, and it became time for a more radical change.

For 2005, a new 987-series Boxster family was launched featuring a completely new body, more powerful engines developing 237bhp (240PS) (Boxster) and 276bhp (280PS) (Boxster S), a new six-speed gearbox for the 'S', uprated running gear and several new options including the active damping control (PASM) and PCCB ceramic disc brakes (Boxster S only). Running costs were reduced by the increase of the inspection and oil change intervals from 12,500 to 18,500 miles.

STYLING

Ever since Porsche cars have existed, the development of existing models has always been evolutionary, rather than revolutionary. In the case of the second generation Boxster,

Porsche has stuck to this successful policy. It has also stuck to the policy which, in the mid-90s, made the Boxster possible: sharing the largest possible number of parts and components with the 911 family. It is consequently not surprising that as the 996-series 911 evolved into the 997-series so the evolution of the 986 Boxster followed the same lines, leading to the 987, which is instantly identifiable as a Porsche Boxster, even though not a single external body panel has been carried over from the previous model. As with the 997-series 911, the Boxster's track has been increased by 24–35mm depending on the wheels on which it rolls, which are larger and wider than its predecessor's; the wings are marginally higher and wider, increasing the car's overall width

▼ Ghosted view of the 987-series Boxster S with six-speed manual gearbox

▲ The new 987-
series Boxster S

▲ The hood is opened
or closed electrically
in only 12 seconds. It
can now be operated
at speeds up to 30mph.
Three layers of fabric
ensure a cosy interior

by 21mm; and the wheel openings are larger. In contrast the doors are slightly thinner, without reducing the body's internal width, which means that externally the car's centre section is marginally narrower than before and results in a mild 'Coke' bottle shape when seen from above, further emphasised by the sills that protrude to form a lip. The front and rear plastic skirts are all-new, but the Boxster S retains the additional central air intake in addition to the two lateral intakes, which are now larger than before.

The front skirt and the new 'rounded triangle' headlights with separate fog and parking lights are surely the easiest way to quickly identify the new Boxster. The 'Litronic' option is now replaced with the bi-Xenon option in which both the high and low beams are Xenon lights. From the side the larger lateral intakes leading air into the engine bay are instantly noticeable; while from the rear the larger tail lights and the oblique joint line of the rear skirt with the steel body, running down from the top of the tail lights, distinguish the new car from its predecessor.

▼ The moulded body side panels are highlighted in this view of a Boxster 2.7

▲ The dashboard
was completely
redesigned for the
987-series Boxster

INTERIOR

The biggest improvement in the cabin is surely the provision
of a fully-adjustable steering column, manual up-and-down
adjustment over a range of 40mm having been added
to the existing axial adjustment. The standard 375mm
(14¾in) diameter steering wheel is new while a similar sized
multifunction wheel carrying the buttons controlling the sound
system and a 370mm 'sport' steering wheel are options. All
three wheels have a lightweight magnesium structure. Tall
drivers will be happy to learn that a new design of the scuttle
has made it possible to move the accelerator and brake
pedals 10mm forward and the clutch pedal 15mm forward,
while the floor has been modified to increase the lowest seat
position by 20mm.

The dashboard and centre console have been completely
redesigned. They are very similar to the 997-series 911's and
include a large glovebox in front of the passenger's seat. Their
surface finish is achieved by a 'slush' moulding process, giving
an appearance very similar to leather and offers a pleasant soft
touch. Real leather is an option.

The instrument cluster includes three larger and less overlapping dials than before with, as usual, the rev counter in the middle. The analogue speedometer is on the left and the dial on the right includes the fuel and water temperature guages. A digital speedometer is included in the rev counter dial, while the speedometer dial houses trip and overall mileage recorders. Time, outside temperature and on-board computer displays are included in the right-hand dial. The rest of the functions are checked by LED warning lamps. The dials are black with white digits in the Boxster and light grey with red digits in the Boxster S. The best part of the centre console is taken up by the standard air conditioning and the sound and infotainment systems, or by the optional navigation system. It also carries the inevitable retractable cup holder and various non-priority switches, such as the switch cutting off the PSM electronic stability system, now standard even on the basic Boxster, or that selecting the sport mode of the optional PASM suspension.

Manual air conditioning is now standard in both the Boxster and Boxster S, and pollen and active carbon filters have been added. Automatic air conditioning is an option.

▲ The instrument cluster of the 987-series Boxster S retains the light grey dials, but they are larger and more legible than before

The well-shaped new standard seats, of which the backrest has been extended by 50mm for better head protection in the case of a rear crash, provide excellent lateral hold. They are electrically adjustable for seat angle and backrest inclination, their longitudinal position and height being manually adjustable for weight reasons. A lightweight sport seat with the same adjustments but 50 per cent more lateral hold is also available and 12-way fully electrically adjustable normal and sport seats are optional.

The electric hood mechanism has been further developed. After manually releasing the clamp securing the hood to the upper windscreen rail, the hood can now be opened and closed in about 12 seconds (as before) without stopping the car by simply pushing a button on the horizontal console, provided the speed does not exceed 30mph. To further improve the thermal and noise insulation, a second layer of internal lining has been added.

PASSIVE SAFETY

Several measures have further improved the passive safety of the Boxster. One is a further increase of the body's torsional and beam rigidity which is achieved by Porsche's new sheet metal assembly technique. Starting with the 997 (911) and 987 (Boxster) series models, the body's side panels are bonded to the floorpan as well as spot-welded. This has resulted in a nine per cent improvement in the torsional resistance to 12,200Nm/ degree with the top closed and a 14 per cent improvement in beam resistance. Better frontal and offset-frontal crash safety is achieved by a longitudinal high-resistance steel profile added in the upper part of the door. This helps transmit the impact forces from the upper level of the front structure, through the doors,

▼ Six airbags and two roll bars take care of the occupants' safety

to the rear part of the body, for the best possible energy absorption. In addition, as in the 997-series 911, the entire front bulkhead has been redesigned with a widespread use of very high resistant steel, both to move the pedals forward and to improve rigidity and crash safety.

The new Boxster is also the first roadster to feature six airbags: there are two frontal bags plus two bags contained in the seat backrests and two bags contained in the doors just below the window sill, rising to prevent head injuries in the case of a side impact. The roll-over bars behind the seats are now made of stainless steel and have been raised 25mm, compared to the earlier models. They have also been moved back 31mm to increase the storage space behind the seats.

To compensate for the weight added by the more rigid structure and the new safety features, Porsche has decided to

▼ The various
materials used in
the body structure

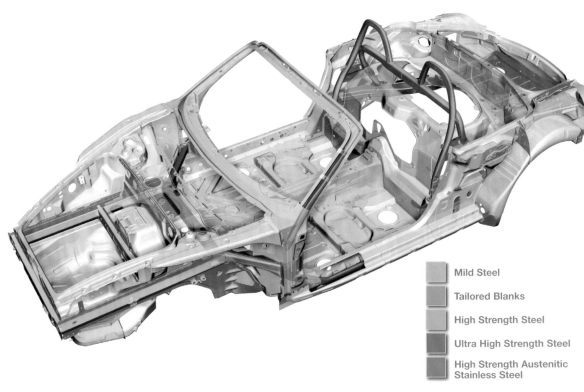

Mild Steel

Tailored Blanks

High Strength Steel

Ultra High Strength Steel

High Strength Austenitic
Stainless Steel

make the front and rear boot lids in aluminium, a saving of 9kg, and to delete the spare wheel and jack; these are replaced with a tyre repair kit and an electric air compressor, saving 10kg (22lb). Following the deletion of the spare wheel, the capacity of the front luggage compartment is increased from 130 to 150 litres. As the rear boot size has not changed, the total luggage capacity under cover is now 280 litres.

▲ A perfectly flat bottom contributes to the Boxster's low drag and low lift figures

AERODYNAMIC DEVELOPMENTS

The new Boxster generation has a marginally larger frontal area than its predecessors. Mainly due to its wider tyres and wings, it has increased from 1.94m² to 1.96m² (1.97m² for the Boxster S), but a reduction of the drag coefficient (C_d) from 0.31 to 0.29 for the Boxster and from 0.32 to 0.30 for the Boxster S more than compensates for the increased frontal area, the total drag factor resulting in (C_dxS = 0.29x1.96=) 0.57 for the Boxster and 0.59

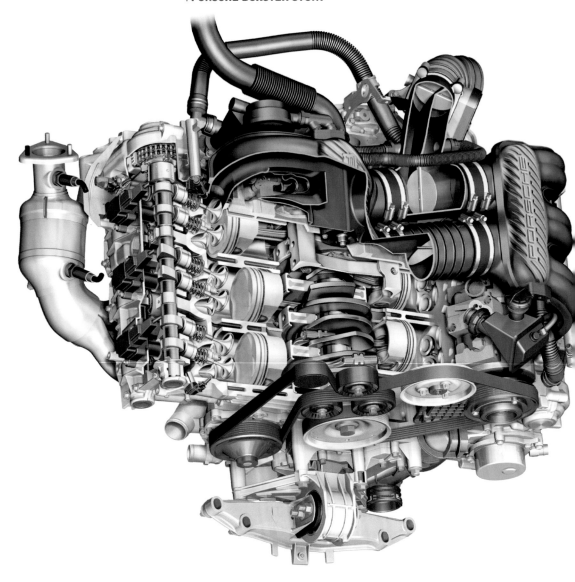

▲ The 3.2-litre M96/26
engine of the 987-series
Boxster S develops
276bhp (280PS), 236lb ft
(320Nm) of torque and
weighs 197kg

for the Boxster S. The overall lift coefficient has been lowered
from 0.22 for the 986 series to 0.16 for the 987 series, front lift
being reduced by 25 per cent and rear lift by 30 per cent.

Several measures have contributed to these improvements.
The underbody is now completely flat, thanks to the addition of
a number of lightweight plastic panels; the front end of the car
has been designed to avoid air rushing into the wheelarches;
the front-bumper ducts leading cooling air to the radiators and
the front brakes have been completely redesigned for better
aerodynamic efficiency and to reduce the lift generating pressure
build-up inside the wheel housings.

ENGINE DEVELOPMENTS

The increase in engine performance that came with the introduction of the second generation Boxster family was achieved without any increase in cubic capacity, solely by redesigning the intake and exhaust system for better efficiency. These modifications raised the power and torque of the 2.7 engine (now M96/25) from 225bhp (228PS) to 237bhp (240PS) and from 192lb ft (260Nm) to 199lb ft (270Nm) respectively while in the 3.2-litre engine (now M96/26), the power was increased from 256bhp (260PS) to 276bhp (280PS) and the torque from 229lb ft (310Nm) to 236lb ft (320Nm). The engines themselves remained essentially unchanged, except for the addition of a vacuum pump driven from the right-hand exhaust camshaft. This was found desirable because, with the high rate of exhaust gas recirculation required to meet exhaust emission requirements and pumping losses under certain circumstances the vacuum created in the intake manifold was insufficient for reliable operation of the brake servo and other vacuum-operated devices.

▼ Comparison of power and torque curves of Boxster engines; model years 2004 (dashed) and 2005

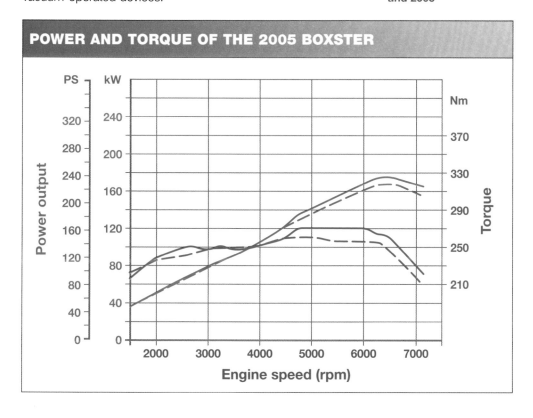

POWER AND TORQUE OF THE 2005 BOXSTER

Cams, valve timing, valve sizes and lift remained unchanged, only the Variocam programme being slightly revised. A minor modification to the 3.2-litre engine was the use of reinforced pistons which added 12g to their weight, two thirds of which was compensated by drilling the gudgeon pins conically at either end, saving 8g – more important than it sounds in an engine revving up to 7,200rpm!

5.5kg was saved on the 2.7-litre engine by deleting the cast-iron bearing supports in the vertically-split aluminium main bearing block. The reason for the cast-iron inlays was to reduce bearing clearance variations due to the high heat expansion coefficient of aluminium. At the development stage of the engine it was found that at high engine temperatures the grip on the bearing shells could be reduced to the point that the shells turned in their seat. In the continuing effort to reduce weight and costs, experiments with an all-aluminium bearing block were resumed and it was found that increasing the bearing shell thickness from 2.5mm to 3mm made it possible to delete the cast iron bearing supports, at least in the smaller of the two engines.

▼ Comparison of power and torque curves of Boxster S engines; model years 2004 (dashed) and 2005

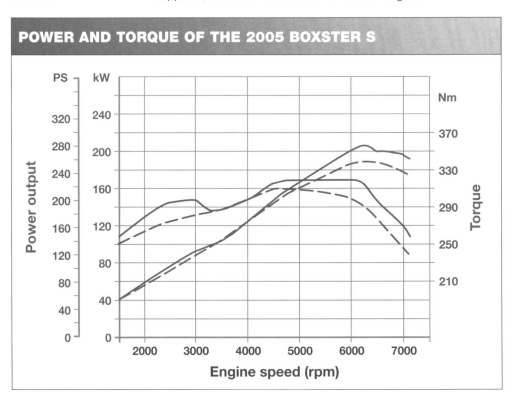

POWER AND TORQUE OF THE 2005 BOXSTER S

COOLING SYSTEM

The higher power output of the two engines has required
increased cooling, obtained by the use of radiators of five per
cent increased area and a 20 per cent thicker core and more
powerful fans, now with infinitely-variable speed control. Boxster
S models with Tiptronic S transmission have a third, centrally-
located radiator feeding the oil/water intercooler for the gearbox.

INTAKE AND EXHAUST SYSTEMS

Better breathing is the key to increased power and starts with
an air filter of much increased surface compared with previous
models, which minimises the pressure drop across the filter. The
increased surface also requires less frequent changes of the
filter element, Porsche recommending a change after 60,000km
(37,000 miles) instead of 20,000km (12,500 miles) previously.
Past the air mass meter and the throttle valve, the intake pipe
is longitudinally divided in two paths leading to the cross tube
feeding the right and left plenum chambers, from which the two
cylinder banks draw air. As before, the two plenum chambers
are further linked by a second tube, the resonance pipe,

▲ The new design of
side air intake for the
987-series Boxster

controlled by a butterfly valve which, at low engine speeds, remains closed. Where the longitudinally-divided pipe joins the cross tube is another butterfly valve, called the 'distributor valve', which, when vertical (closed), blocks any communication between the two cylinder banks so that the flow of air in the divided pipe is split, one half feeding one bank, the other half feeding the other bank of cylinders. This is what happens at low engine speeds, when each cylinder bank draws air from what amounts to a long pipe, favouring a good torque.

Around 1,500rpm, the distributor valve moves to its horizontal (open) position, opening the communication between the two plenum chambers. When the engine speed reaches 3,000rpm (Boxster S: 3,500rpm), the distributor valve moves back to its vertical (closed) position, splitting the air flow to the two cylinder banks again. At the same time, the resonance valve opens, and the movement of the intake air in the system generates pressure waves creating a supercharging effect. Above 5,600rpm (Boxster S: 5,500rpm), the distributor valve opens again and both cross pipes are now open to match the frequency of the pressure waves to the higher engine speed. The result is to retain the torque at its maximum level all the way between 4,700 and 6,000rpm. The valves of the system are operated by vacuum capsules under control of the Bosch 7.8 engine management system, which has increased computing power and the additional tasks of controlling the new manifold flap of the twin branch system, the steplessly-controlled radiator fan speed and, if fitted, the Sport Chrono Package.

The optimisation of the engine's breathing is continued in the exhaust system, which has been completely revised. Thin wall (1.2mm instead of 1.5mm) stainless steel pipes of increased diameter ensure low weight and a free flow of the exhaust gases. To help meet the EU 4 and the American LEV II regulations, pre-catalysts are integrated in the two exhaust manifolds where they reach their operating temperature within the shortest possible time after a cold start. The 3.2-litre engine gets new high performance manifolds with three equal length tuned pipes. Leaving the manifold, the exhaust pipes are led through the wheelarches to the twin wall rear silencers incorporating the main catalysts. These are connected by a

▼ **The resonance intake manifold of the 987-series Boxster. This illustration shows the distributor valve (furthest from the camera) controlling the flow of air in the divided intake pipe. When the valve is vertical, each channel of the divided intake pipe feeds one cylinder bank separately. When it is horizontal, the two banks communicate. In the foreground is the resonance valve, which controls the resonance pipe**

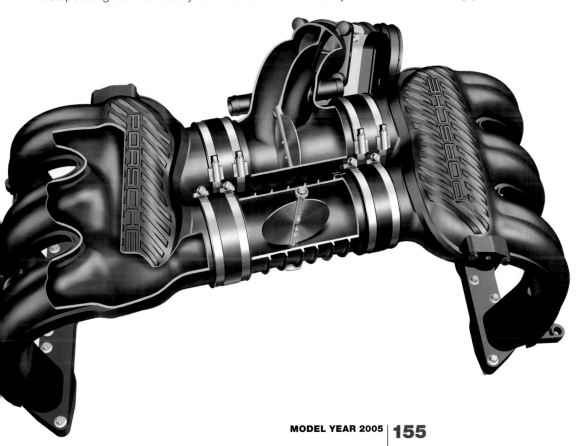

cross-over pipe from which the exhaust gas is fed to the single oval tail pipe of the Boxster or to the twin tail pipes of the Boxster S. The core of the catalysts is now ceramic which is lighter than metal. Compared to the previous model, 4kg is saved on the exhaust system despite the added pre-catalysts.

Great care has also been taken to retain and even improve the typical 'Porsche sound' of the engine. For this, both the intake and the exhaust systems are relevant, the length and diameter of the various pipes being of paramount importance in this respect. A Helmholtz resonator has even been added in the air filter housing to eliminate disturbing high frequency peaks.

TRANSMISSION DEVELOPMENTS

For 2005 the basic Boxster retains its five-speed manual gearbox, with improved synchromesh, but the six-speed manual box of the Boxster S is entirely new.

The five-speed Tiptronic S transmissions, optional with both the 2.7-litre and 3.2-litre engines, are developments of the previous units, adapted to transmit the increased torque of the more powerful engines.

THE G87/00 FIVE-SPEED MANUAL GEARBOX

The five-speed manual gearbox of the 987-series Boxster was a development of the previous unit. Instead of featuring single cone synchromesh on all gears, first gear gets a triple-cone synchroniser and second gear a double-cone device. These reduce the shifting time and the force required for shifting and has made it possible to reduce the gear lever travel by 27 per cent for quicker shifts.

In view of the larger rolling radius of the driving wheels (324mm instead of 310mm), the final-drive ratio has been raised from 3.56:1 to 3.75:1, the five internal gear ratios having remained unchanged. This results in a speed of 24mph at 1,000rpm in top gear.

THE G87/20 SIX-SPEED MANUAL GEARBOX

The high torque of the 2005 model 3.2-litre engines required a gearbox of higher torque capacity than used in earlier models. The new 'box, produced by Getrag to Porsche's specifications, has triple-cone synchromesh on first and second gears and double-cone synchromesh on the four

G87/20 MANUAL GEARBOX RATIOS	
Gear	Ratio
1st	3.667: 1
2nd	2.050: 1
3rd	1.407: 1
4th	1.133: 1
5th	0.972: 1
6th	0.822: 1
Reverse	3.33: 1
Final drive: 3.875:1	

upper gears, for quicker shifts, and led to a 15 per cent reduction in gear lever travel. The gear ratios are different throughout from those of the earlier six-speed gearbox, but while the overall gearing (gear ratio x final drive ratio) in first gear is clearly 'shorter' than before, second, third and fourth gears are very similar, while fifth and sixth are 'shorter' than in the previous 'box to compensate for the greater rolling radius of the new Boxster family's wheels.

THE TIPTRONIC S TRANSMISSIONS

The A87/01 transmission of the 2.7-litre Boxster and the A87/20 transmission of the 3.2-litre Boxster S, both made by ZF and known as 'Tiptronic S' in Porsche language, are basically carried over from earlier models. 'Tiptronic S' implies an automatic transmission with a highly adaptive programme developed by Porsche, with provision for manual control by steering wheel mounted trigger switches even when the automatic programme has been selected. More details about the function of the electronic programmes of the Tiptronic and Tiptronic S transmissions can be obtained in the 'Transmission' sections for the 1997 and 2000 models.

Both transmissions have been adapted to the increased power and torque of the engines, mainly by raising the pressure with which the clutches and brakes of the epicyclic gear sets are operated, while the automatic shift programme has been modified for better adaptation to uphill and downhill slopes. A probably more important modification is the 'shorter' gearing of the final drive. Together with the increased power of the engines, this modification gives better in-gear acceleration, especially in the case of the lower-powered 2.7-litre model. The car's speed at 1,000rpm is now 24mph for the Boxster and 26.4mph for the Boxster S, maximum speed being reached in fifth gear.

A new lower viscosity fluid is now used in both transmissions, reducing power absorption while increasing fluid change intervals from 100,000 to 112,000 miles.

▼ Boxster S cockpit with optional leather upholstery

▲ New front axle with redesigned cross-member and hollow wheel carriers, both in pressure-cast aluminium

RUNNING GEAR, STEERING AND DRIVING AIDS

Basically, the running gear of the 987 series Boxster family is similar to that of its predecessors, but none of its components has remained unchanged. Front and rear tracks are wider thanks to 30mm wider crossmembers, now pressure cast, further improving the car's stability and handling. With standard wheels, the front and rear tracks of the Boxster are increased by 25mm and 30mm respectively, those of the Boxster S by 31mm and 15mm, the differences being due to different wheel rim offsets. The front crossmember has been redesigned and the anti-roll bar moved above the crossmember for better offset crash safety. In addition several highly-stressed components, such as the front and rear wheel carriers, have been redesigned in view of the increased performance and of the increased grip of the latest tyres. Instead of being plain aluminium sand castings, they are now hollow aluminium pressure-die-castings for greater strength and lower weight, designed to take wheel bearings of 80mm instead of 75mm diameter.

For better absorption of road-induced vibrations, the rubber bush on which the front longitudinal suspension arms of the McPherson front suspension are pivoted are replaced with hydraulically-damped bushes, while, for better crash resistance, the anti-roll bar is moved from its position ahead of the transverse member to a position above it. At the rear, the wheel carriers are now common to the Boxster and Boxster S, meaning that the Boxster now benefits from the longer track levers (part of the upright) introduced on the Boxster S for the 2000 model year.

▼ Rear axle of the 987-series Boxster with new cross-member and hollow wheel carriers in pressure-cast aluminium

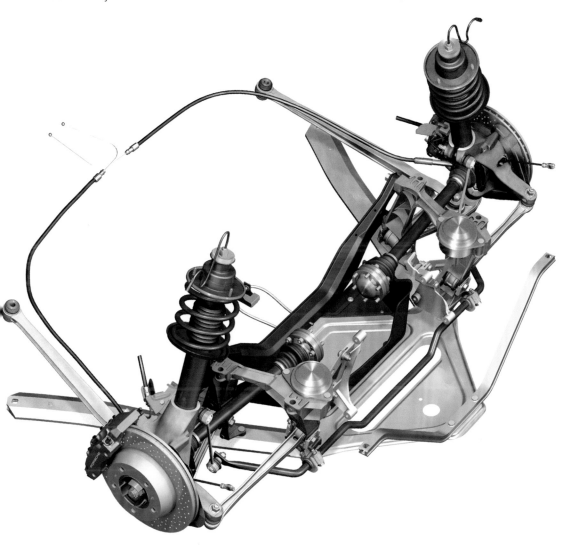

SUSPENSION DATA

BOXSTER	front	rear
Spring rate at wheel (N/mm)	27	30
Dampers	two-tubes, gas filled	
Frequency, no load (Hz)	1.6	1.55
Tubular anti-roll bar, dia x thickness (mm)	23.6 x 3.4	19.0 x 2.5

BOXSTER S	front	rear
Spring rate at wheel (N/mm)	27	33
Dampers	two-tubes, gas filled	
Frequency, no load (Hz)	1.59	1.6
Tubular anti-roll bar, dia x thickness (mm)	24 x 3.8	19.6 x 2.6

BOXSTER S PASM	front	rear
Spring rate at wheel (N/mm)	33	40
Dampers	two-tubes, gas filled	
Frequency, no load (Hz)	1.7	1.72
Tubular anti-roll bar, dia x thickness (mm)	24.5 x 3.8	19.6 x 2.6

The spring rates of the standard suspension are about ten per cent higher than for the 986-series Boxster and Boxster S. The anti-roll bars are also slightly stiffer.

PASM

The Porsche Active Suspension management was introduced to combine the comfort of the standard running gear with the uprated handling provided by the 'Sport' running gear offered on 986-series Boxsters.

The ride height of cars equipped with PASM is 10mm lower than standard. Two modes are provided by a dash-mounted switch: 'Normal' and 'Sport'. In the 'Normal' position, PASM provides a really comfortable low speed ride – in the author's opinion, more comfortable than the standard suspension – but as the speed increases, the damping is progressively increased to match the handling to the driving conditions.

The 'Sport' mode increases the damping force noticeably

from low speeds and, as it further increases with the car's speed, it is best suited to hard driving on well surfaced roads and to track work. It also reduces the sensitivity of the PSM, which intervenes later before overriding the driver's action in case, for example, of a power slide.

▲ A Boxster S on this sort of road is at its best

PASM consists of the following components:
- Four dampers of continuously variable damping force controlled by a by-pass valve;
- The PASM electronic control unit;
- Two acceleration sensors sensing the body movements (one on top of the right-hand front damper dome, one on top of the left-hand rear damper dome); and
- A switch for the selection of the required programme.

The other data required for the function of the PASM – the lateral acceleration, the steering column angle, the car's speed

and the brake pressure – are transmitted to the PASM control unit from the PSM (Porsche Stability Management) unit; the engine torque by the DME engine management unit.

Each damper is controlled separately by the PASM control unit. In both the 'Sport' and 'Normal' modes, the damping force increases not only with the car's speed but also responds to a hard acceleration or deceleration to reduce squat or dive, or to quick lane changes, avoiding actions and fast cornering to reduce transient roll. If PASM recognises a poor road surface, however, the damping is instantly reduced for better comfort or to avoid wheel tramp. Alternatively, if excessive vertical movements are sensed, as can happen on undulating roads, damping is automatically increased.

THE SPORT CHRONO PLUS

The Sport Chrono Plus Kit is an option on both the Boxster and Boxster S. It operates in connection with the PASM and includes an analogue and digital timer on a swivel mounting on top of the dashboard, so that it can also be read by a passenger. Activated by pushing the steering-column switch axially, it has been developed to enable the driver to time himself easily on a racing circuit. The lap times can be read instantly, but are also memorised to be easily recalled after the drive. The laps can also be visualised graphically on the PCM (Porsche Communication Module) screen. The Sport Chrono Plus also intervenes in the engine management and in the PASM programmes; in Tiptronic-equipped cars also in the shift programme, to create the best possible conditions, even surpassing the stage of the 'Sport' programme, for a good performance:

With the Sport Chrono Plus activated:
- the throttle valve reacts faster and less progressively to the accelerator pedal movements
- the rev limiter intervenes slightly later, but less progressively
- the PASM is switched automatically into the 'Sport' mode
- in Tiptronic cars, the upshifts and downshifts take place at higher speeds

▼ The Sport Chrono timer is located centrally on top of the dashboard

▲ The Boxster rolls on 17in light alloy wheels. Its 298mm ventilated front brake discs are now perforated. 18in and 19in wheels are optional

WHEELS AND TYRES

With the 987-series come increased contact patches of the tyres on the road surface, thanks to one inch larger diameter standard wheels, wider rims and appropriate tyres. The standard fittings (rim offset given as 'RO') are now as follows:

Boxster
Front   6.5J x 17 RO 55 with 205/55 ZR 17 tyres
Rear   8J x 17 RO 40 with 235/50 ZR 17 tyres

Boxster S
Front   8J x 18 RO 57 with 235/40 ZR 18 tyres
Rear   9J x 18 RO 43 with 265/40 ZR 18 tyres

Optionally, the Boxster 2.7-litre can be ordered with the same size and style of 18in wheels and tyres as the Boxster S, and both the 2.7-litre and 3.2-litre models can also be ordered with the following super sports set of wheels and tyres:

Front   8J x 19 RO 57 with 235/35 ZR 19 tyres
Rear   9.5J x 19 RO 46 with 265/35 ZR 19 tyres

For winter use, wheels and tyre sizes are unchanged, except that with the 19in wheels the recommended size for the winter tyres is 255/35 R 19. Deleting the spare wheel and jack and replacing them with a repair kit saved 10kg.

STEERING

The 987-series models feature a new steering rack, although hydraulic assistance is the same in principle to that of the 986-series. The novelty is the variable steering ratio obtained by the new steering rack of which the distance between its teeth increases progressively at either end. Around the straight ahead position, the overall ratio is 17.11:1, almost equal with the ratio of the 986-series (16.9:1), which is low geared enough to avoid undesired deviations from the desired line. But as the steering wheel is turned by more than about 30°, the ratio is progressively reduced to 13.76:1 near full lock. Only 2.6 turns are now required from lock to lock instead of three, though it should be noted that because of the larger wheels, the turning circle has increased from 10.6m to 10.9m.

▼ 18in light alloy wheels are standard on the Boxster S. The front 318mm brake discs are unchanged from the 986-series. 19in wheels are an option

▼ PCCB 350mm ceramic brake discs with a new ventilating vane design and six-piston front callipers are an expensive option on the Boxster S. They are immune to fading, are half the weight of cast iron and last three to four times longer

To improve the crash safety and to compensate for the weight of the system, the steering column tubes and the components of the more complicated column height adjustment system are all in aluminium or magnesium.

BRAKES

On the base Boxster the diameter of the rear discs has been increased to 299mm, with unchanged 20mm thickness. As with the Boxster S, these discs are now perforated and in both models 30 per cent larger air deflectors carried by the front

suspension longitudinal link, lead more cooling air to the front brakes. In addition, the multiplying factor of the vacuum servo has been increased by 18 per cent and constant and immediate response under all conditions is now ensured by the new engine-driven vacuum pump.

The Boxster S can now be ordered with the PCCB ceramic brake discs, which, compared with the earlier pattern, feature modified internal ventilating vanes which reduce brake squeal. The PCCB discs have a diameter of 350mm and come with six-piston yellow-painted aluminium callipers at the front and four-piston callipers at the rear. They are exceptionally resistant to fade and wear, and have a higher friction coefficient than cast-iron discs, which improves their response and reduces the pedal effort; additionally they are nearly 50 per cent lighter.

▲ The revised brake cooling air flow of the 987-series also reduces aerodynamic lift, compared to the 986-series

PERFORMANCE

Though Porsche insists that the performance of the Boxster family will always deliberately be kept below 911 levels, performance is a relative notion and the Boxsters are fast and lively cars in their own right. According to Porsche's own figures,

▲ The flowing lines of
the Boxster family are
also utterly functional

the 987-series Boxster S accelerates from rest to 99.5mph (160km/h) in exactly the same time of 12.3 seconds as the last of the 993-series 911s and its time of 24.9sec for the standing start kilometre is only 0.3sec longer.

The 987-series Boxster 2.7's maximum speed of 159mph is 10mph faster than the original 2.5 litre Boxster's and its 6.2sec time to 62mph (100km/h) is 0.7sec shorter. More impressive is the gain of 1.2sec over the standing start kilometre, from 27.4sec to 26.2sec.

Compared to the original Boxster S, the maximum speed of the 987-series has increased from 161mph to 167mph, while the time to reach 100mph from rest has decreased from 13.8sec to 12.3sec. All these figures are for cars with the manual gearbox.

The ultimate judge of a sports car's ability however, is the famous 13 mile (21km) long Nordschleife of the Nürburgring, where Porsche's star tester, former rally World Champion and endurance racer Walter Röhrl, achieved the following lap times:

986-series Boxster 2.7   8min 42sec
986-series Boxster S   8min 31sec (−11sec)

987-series Boxster 2.7   8min 27sec
987-series Boxster S   8min 18sec (−9sec)

   It should be noted that the 987-series Boxster S lap time is only 3 seconds slower than the best time achieved by the same driver at the wheel of a 997-series Carrera 3.6 Coupé.

ACCELERATION AND PERFORMANCE FIGURES

	Boxster Manual	Tiptonic S	Boxster S Manual	Tiptonic S
0–100km/h (0–62mph)	6.2sec	7.1sec	5.5sec	6.3sec
0–160km/h (0–100mph)	14.5sec	16.4sec	12.3sec	13.9sec
0–200km/h (0–124mph)	24.6sec	27.2sec	20.2sec	23.3sec
0–1,000m	26.2sec	27.2sec	24.9sec	25.9sec
Max speed (km/h)	256	250	268	260
(mph)	159	156	166.5	162
Fuel consumption EU norm, overall (mpg)	29.6	27.0	27.3	25.8

The 2005 model

As usual, the German *Auto Motor und Sport* was the first
magazine to publish a full road test of the Boxster, in this case
a Boxster S in its 24 November 2004 issue. After commenting
favourably on the typical Porsche evolutionary development
of the model, Bernd Stegemann writes: "When looking at the
performance figures it becomes obvious that the required
targets have been reached. 100km/h (62mph) comes up in
5.4 seconds instead of 5.7 seconds and by the time 200km/h
(124mph) has been reached, 1.9 seconds have been saved.
Even in 6th gear, the engine displays clearly better flexibility

◀ On right-hand drive cars, the ignition key is on the right of the dash board. The light grey instruments identify a Boxster S

than before, 80–120km/h (50–75mph) in 8.3 seconds is a whole class better than its predecessor's 11.4 seconds. Even from the lowest rpm, the engine pulls strongly and leaves an impression of inexhaustible breath. On a clear road it is difficult not to push it beyond 6,000rpm, if only because of the enthralling acoustics. But in reality it is the incredible smoothness, this clean surge forward that makes Boxster motoring so special.

"The grip is even better than before and the Boxster can be driven around corners as if the laws of physics did not apply to it ... The dynamics are further enhanced by the (optional) extremely

▼ Boxster (left) and Boxster S (right)

grippy 19 inch Michelin tyres specially developed for Porsche, and also by the (optional) PASM active damping system which lowers the Boxster by 10mm and stiffens the suspension automatically when the car is cornered fast. Away from a racing circuit, its abilities can hardly be exploited, but if the 'sport' mode is switched on [on] normal roads, a very accurate feedback of road conditions is provided, much to the discomfort of the passengers. In contrast to this, the light variable-ratio rack-and-pinion steering now absorbs most of the disturbing road inputs and also demonstrates that the improvements made are not necessarily welcome. The spontaneous, almost instinctive response to small corrections around the straight-ahead position has given way to a hint of delay. Only with increasing lock and speed does the old precision and feedback reappear."

Auto Motor und Sport concludes: "The new Boxster S is more Porsche than ever: more powerful, more dynamic and generally more competent. Comfort and cockpit quality have also been noticeably improved. Not optimal are the many little switches and knobs

▼ The spoiler reduces rear lift by over 30 per cent. It is raised automatically at 75mph and retracted when the speed drops below 50mph

and the less spontaneous steering." Nevertheless *Auto Motor und Sport* gives the Boxster S five stars out of five.

    Autocar was among the first British magazines to publish a full road test of a second generation Boxster, a base 2.7-model with fairly comprehensive optional equipment including 18in wheels and bi-Xenon lights, bringing up the kerb weight to 1,360kg. Commenting on the car's restyling, *Autocar* writes "We'd stop well short of calling it ugly, but feel that though its more svelte, wider stance, better detailing and its curvaceous lines improve somewhat on the looks of the original, the update is less successful than the excellent work that turned the 996 into the 997..." Commenting on the performance, the testers said: "... more worrying [is] the fact that it is not exactly going to scare its rivals from BMW and Mercedes either. The 3.0 litres Z4 and SLK 350 will run in considerably less than 6.0sec to 60mph, a feat that proved beyond the Boxster at the test track, despite the considerable advantage of mid-engine traction. The problem is not power which betters the BMW (if not the Mercedes) but torque which trails far behind both. It hits 60mph in 6.1sec, a scant 0.2 seconds quicker than the predecessor.

▲ Like its predecessor, the second-generation Boxster S is clearly identified by the rear boot script

"There's further disappointment in the gearbox ... It was not only possible, but worryingly easy to snag first instead of third when accelerating hard up through the ratios. ... Thank heaven", added the testers, "when the little flat-6 is on song, forgiveness of its other limitations come free and fast. The yowl could only be Porsche, the smoothness at the 7,200rpm red line something which many manufacturers would struggle to match with twice the cylinders.

"Find the right road and you won't need five minutes to know that this is one of the finest-handling cars on sale at any price. In fact it's devilishly hard to fault: it resists understeer with an iron will, yet tolerates mid-corner changes of plan better than any mid-engined car has a right to do. But the real star turns are the damping and the steering. It's one thing for a car to rule its body over ever-changing surfaces, gradients and cambers with such unquestioning authority, but something else to achieve this with such deftness that magnificent ride quality is provided too."

The body still comes in for some criticism for its 'meagre equipment', even though automatic air conditioning is now

▼ When closed, the drag coefficient (C_d) of 0.29 and 0.30 for the Boxster and Boxster S respectively is exceptional for a soft top two-seater

standard. But coming back to the chassis in their conclusions, the testers write: "We find its sublime chassis handsomely rewards the time and effort required and, once on the boil, the engine too. The badge will ensure it attracts its fair share of posers, but we feel they'd be better served in one of the better-looking, more relaxing rivals. The Boxster should be left to proper drivers, those who care more about the fine nuances of its responses than what those next door think."

In the end *Autocar* gives the Boxster four-and-a-half out of a maximum five stars and name it their choice against five competitors in the £26,000–34,000 price bracket.

In a twin test comparing the 987-series Boxster S to the Mercedes-Benz SLK 350, the Belgo-French *Le Moniteur Automobile* writes: "Against the clock, the Porsche's 5kg/PS power to weight ratio makes it the faster-accelerating car, with a standing start kilometre covered in 24.9 seconds compared to the Mercedes' 5.4kg/PS and still highly respectable 25.5 seconds to cover the kilometre ... Where handling is concerned, there are two points where the Porsche is clearly ahead.

One is the new, diabolically accurate variable ratio steering which is a delight and provides superb feedback. It is ideal on winding roads, though the increasingly quicker ratio when the steering wheel angle exceeds 30° requires getting used to if the car is pushed enough to start drifting ... Understeer is almost absent but, driven on a racing circuit, the Boxster displays the typical behaviour of mid-engined cars: incredible grip, but scant progressivity as the limit is reached, requiring prompt and accurate action if grip is broken.

"The second discipline in which the new Porsche shines is braking. The further improved brakes are not only astonishingly powerful, but equally progressive and fade resistant, as Porsche brakes have been for so many years."

The author, Pascal Binon, concludes as follows: "Featuring more (too many) driving aids than the Boxster, the SLK is a very dynamic and practical roadster with a big boot and a retractable rigid top, while the Boxster S is a real sports car appealing to all the senses of its driver through its fabulous combination of engine, transmission and chassis. Lucky Porschistes!"

▼ The navigation
system is a useful option

In its March 2005 issue, *Road & Track* evaluated nine sports cars for their all-round abilities. The cars – in alphabetical order BMW Z4, Corvette C6 Coupé, Dodge Viper roadster, Honda S2000, Lotus Elise, Mercedes-Benz SLK350, Nissan 350Z Anniversary, Porsche Boxster S and Porsche Carrera S – were driven both on public roads and on a race track and assessed for acceleration – 0–60mph and standing quarter-mile – fuel economy, slalom and skid-pad performance, handling, steering, braking, styling, luggage space, driving excitement and, of course, price. The judges were seven *Road & Track* journalists and Steve Millen, a former IMSA racing champion. On merit only, excluding the price, the Carrera S comes out the winner, closely followed by the Boxster, which won the slalom contest, the braking contest (sharing the laurels with the Carrera S) and also won for exterior styling, seat comfort (again shared with the Carrera S), ergonomics (shared with four other cars). Taking the price into consideration, it is not a surprise to see the Corvette, which took third place, top the list, followed by the Boxster S and Carrera S in second and third spots.

▲ In the front view the second-generation Boxster (here an S) is much more elegant than its forerunner, mainly thanks to its new headlights

▲ The sidelights and indicators were separated from the main headlamps for the second-generation Boxster

Commenting on the Boxster S, the *Road & Track* testers said: "This German two-seater won as many categories as its [Carrera S] stablemate [five] and nearly walked away with the overall prize. And as far as the *R&T* editors were concerned it was the winner – five out of eight of them put it at the top of their lists. Whether at the track or on public roads, the Boxster S enthralled all who sat in its plush leather seats.

"The new iteration is a wonderful sports car, now with a bit more style and power. The engine revs wonderfully and pulls strongly through the rev bands. The gearbox is excellent and though there is a bit of vertical motion through corners and over rises, once you're used to it there is no problem.

"On the West Loop the Boxster S was a model of balance, with the engine harmoniously in sync with the chassis. The 3.2-litre dohc flat-six revved effortlessly through its rev range. Its generous low- and mid-range torque supplied excellent 'snap' off the line and good speed exiting corners. Stay on the throttle and its acceleration curve gets steeper and steeper, like a thoroughbred on the final stretch. It reached 130mph on the straight and posted the fourth best lap time.

"The basic geometry of the suspension remains unchanged ... but the car feels a bit stiffer than before, thus exhibiting better stability through slow corners. Turn-in is super-crisp, thanks in part to its quick communicative steering. In fact, many of us felt that the Boxster S displayed sharper responses than the 911 Carrera S. And no wonder, the stylish roadster was the fastest through the slalom, putting [up] a record time of 73.9sec (yes, it ousted the Ferrari Enzo!) and it out-braked the rest from 60mph, needing only 107ft of tarmac to a dead stop.

"On the road the car is a delight. Its predictable handling and seamless power delivery make it the ideal mount for winding mountain passes. Ride quality is good and the interior, which is among the cosiest of the group, is comfortable and quiet – it does not get as cacophonous as some of the other soft-tops in this test.

"Where the Boxster S falters is price. Its base sticker of $53,100 will keep it from entering many people's drive-way and it kept the car from taking top honours in this test."

▼ For winter use, a lightweight hard top is an optional extra

Further comments come from the comparison test between the Nissan 350Z Roadster and a Porsche Boxster S published in the May 2005 issue of the Italian magazine *Auto*.

"Wider track and larger wheels further increase the already highly dynamic character of the Boxster S. And as the dynamism increases, the 'racing', near 'professional' feel of the Boxster S, influenced by the central/rear position of the powerful engine and the quick reactions this position creates, emerges clearer than ever. No doubt, the electronic stability system works well, but to feel at home in the Boxster at the speeds it achieves requires precise and adequate reactions on the part of the driver through the car's accurate controls. This is certainly not a fault: it is this sense of control which the typical Porsche driver likes to feel."

The comparison between the two cars – Boxster S and Nissan 350Z Roadster – continues by mentioning that the 290kg lighter Porsche beat the Nissan in the 0–100km/h (0–62mph) sprint by one second and to the 180km/h (112mph) mark by five seconds.

"Luxury, attention to detail and timeless styling make the Boxster S a car in which the contrast between a very warm welcome and the dynamic, even furious, potential reaches

extremes. But they don't disturb nor even trigger an emotional shock. The progressive and highly sensitive steering provides the driver with precise and direct feedback. If the sporting mode of the PASM, which practically eliminates roll, and the 'Sport Chrono' function, which accelerates the throttle response, have been selected then from the driver's seat you can literally feel the road rushing under the wheels, almost unfiltered, while a push on the throttle pedal instantly illustrates the aggressive character of the chassis and engine. If pushed, after an early tendency to understeer at turn-in, the former soon adopts a neutral attitude with a tendency to run wide if the throttle is released. (*) The variations in the car's attitude happen very quickly, depending on the balance between traction and grip. The 3.2-litre engine makes up for its inferior low range torque with a tremendous 'accelerato' between 4,000rpm and 7,000rpm, a fascinating experience. Once experienced, the deep, furious cry of the flat-six, right behind the ears, is unforgettable."

(*) The author disagrees with this statement. The Boxster's lift-off reaction is moderate tuck-in.

CHAPTER 8

The 2005 Cayman S

Eight years of Boxster production had persuaded Porsche that there was a market for a closed car in the Boxster class. Over long distances, open cars become tiring and in the closed position even the best soft tops cause more wind noise than closed bodies. They also offer less luggage space because of the stowage space required for the hood.

Though Porsche want the Cayman to be known as a new range, the elegant coupé body cannot hide the fact that its mechanical layout and the body structure up to the waist line are identical to the Boxster's. The floorpan remains unchanged in spite of the extra stiffness provided by the Cayman's steel roof. This explains how, in spite of its large hatch, the Cayman has a torsional stiffness of 31,500 Nm/degree, about two and a half times higher than the Boxster's and only five per cent less than the 997-series 911's. A high torsional stiffness is very important for the satisfactory interaction of the front and rear suspensions. As for beam stiffness, the Cayman's 16,500 N/mm is twice as high as the Boxster's, which is one of the structurally stiffest models among contemporary open cars. Due to the use of the unmodified Boxster floorpan, the weight of the Cayman, 1,340kg, is only 5kg less than that of the Boxster S.

BODY

Most of the Cayman's body panels are different from the
Boxster's, except for the doors (which it also shares with the
911), the front wings and the aluminium front boot lid. The rear
boot, of which the 260-litre capacity is exactly twice that of the
Boxster's, is accessible through a large hatch. The plastic front
skirt is new and makes the Cayman instantly recognisable from
the front. From the side, the shape is typically Porsche and the
rather domed roof is reminiscent of the 356 coupés, while the
side air intakes with vertical slats (left feeding the engine intake,
right ventilating the engine bay) are higher and shallower than in
the Boxster.

Extensive wind tunnel tests have resulted in a low drag
coefficient of 0.29 and a 50 per cent reduction in front and rear
lift compared with the Boxter. This has been achieved mainly
by the replacement of the Boxter's pop-up rear spoiler by a
so-called split aerofoil. When retracted, it looks like an 85cm
wide and 10cm deep split 'duck's tail' the upper part of which
is raised by 80mm when the car reaches a speed of 75mph.

These views of the Cayman S clearly show that its body is a long way from being just a Boxster with a steel top. The boot takes 260 litres of luggage, in addition to the front compartment's 150 litres, and gives access to the engine

▲ The design of
the 18in wheels
is exclusive to
the Cayman

The raised part is aerofoil shaped and the air flowing through the gap between it and the fixed base creates a downforce opposing the lift, improving the Cayman's high speed stability and grip. The aerofoil retracts when then the car's speed drops below 50mph.

Though the interior layout is almost identical to that of the Boxster, including the instrument panel and the seats, it is more luxuriously trimmed, while the roof liner is Alcantara. There is no separation between the passenger compartment and the rear boot except for a cross rail behind the seats to retain luggage in the event of sharp braking or an accident. The rear boot has two levels: its rear part has a fairly low floor, while the forward part is raised to clear

▼ A beautiful ghosted view of the Cayman S

the engine. The entire compartment is upholstered and highly sound-proofed against engine noise. Luggage nets are provided to secure items and the deeper part of the boot is hidden from view by a removable liner, which is raised as the hatch is opened. An integrated box provides access to the oil and coolant fillers. An oil dipstick is not provided, the level being obtained instead from a dashboard indicator.

THE M97/21 3.4-LITRE ENGINE

The engine of the Cayman S is largely similar to the 997-series 911's M96/05 unit, with the crankshaft's stroke reduced to 78mm, resulting in a capacity of 3,386cc. The reduced stroke and the 3mm larger, 63mm diameter main bearing of the Cayman engine result in an exceptionally stiff crankshaft. The intake system is the same as for the Boxster 2.7 and 3.2 engines and the 11.1:1 compression ratio is marginally higher.

The crossflow cylinder heads are those of the 911 Carrera and feature the latest Variocam Plus intake valve gear in which both the valve timing and lift are variable. The timing variations up to a

▼ Side air intakes of the Cayman S are a slightly different shape to those of the Boxster and have vertical slats

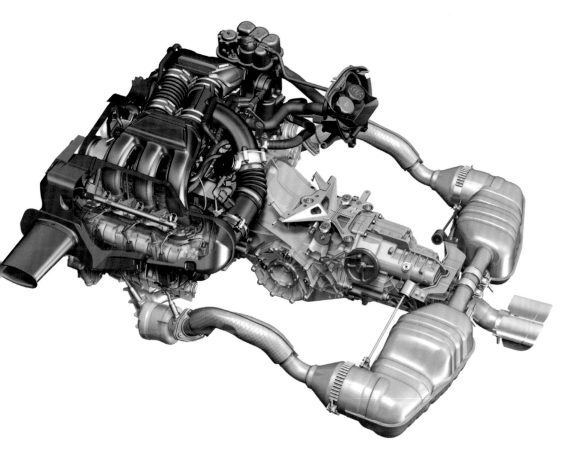

crankshaft angle of 40° are obtained by a hydraulic vane-type cam angle variator while the lift variations are achieved by the use of two concentric inverted cup tappets, separately operated by high and low lift cams. These can operate separately or be connected with each other by a hydraulic plunger. Both the timing and lift variations are governed by the engine management unit (Bosch Motronic 7.8). Intake and exhaust valve diameters are respectively 40.2mm and 34.5mm, and maximum valve lift is 11mm for both.

▲ The complete layout of the 3.4-litre engine and transmission of the Cayman S. Note the oil and coolant fillers, which are accessed from the rear boot

The valve timing is as follows for high lift and 1mm valve clearance:

'Early' timing:	Intake	opens 29° before TDC
		closes 20° after BDC
'Late' timing:	Intake	opens 11° after TDC
		closes 60° after BDC
	Exhaust	opens 50° before BDC
		closes 4.5° before TDC

For low (3.6mm) valve lift and 1mm valve clearance:

'Early' timing: Intake   opens 1° before TDC

closes 59° before BDC

'Late' timing: Intake   opens 39° after TDC

closes 19° before BDC

Exhaust   opens 50° before BDC

closes 4.5° before TDC

This elaborate Variocam Plus enables the Cayman S to meet all current emission regulations worldwide while achieving a high torque over a wide range of engine speeds. A further contribution to clean emissions is the use of new fuel injectors, ensuring finer atomization of the fuel, together with more efficient pre-catalysts than in Boxster engines.

▼ **In terms of performance the Cayman S is pitched between the Boxster S and the 911 Carrera**

The variable intake system, as used on the 2005 Boxster, together with the Variocam Plus valve gear help the engine develop 292bhp (295PS) at 6,250rpm and a maximum torque of 258lb ft (340Nm) between 4,400rpm and 6,000rpm, the maximum permissible crankshaft speed being 7,300rpm.

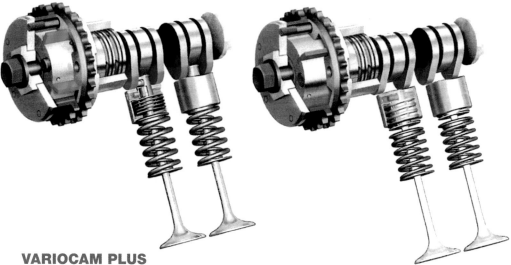

VARIOCAM PLUS

Variocam Plus is made up of a vane-type camshaft angle variator and switchable two-stage inverted cup tappets providing two different valve lift and opening duration modes. It operates only the intake valves.

The vane-type camshaft angle variator, described on pages 127–131 can turn the camshaft up to an angle of 20° resulting in an angle variation of 40° on the valve timing diagram.

The "Plus" in the system governs the valve lift variations. It is entirely incorporated in the two-piece tappets consisting mainly of the high lift tappet, a fairly thick sleeve of 31mm external

▲ **Left: Variocam in low lift mode with cam angle variator in 'early' position. Right: Variocam in high lift mode with cam angle variator in 'late' position**

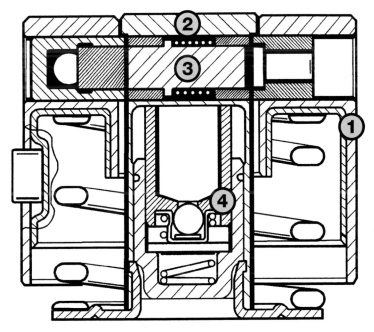

◄ Sectional view of Variocam Plus tappet
1 High lift outer tappet body
2 Inner, low lift tappet containing the zero-lash valve clearance adjuster
3 Plunger linking the inner and outer tappets
4 Zero-lash adjuster

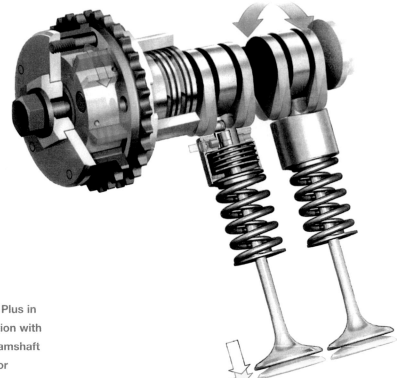

▶ Variocam Plus in
low lift position with
vane-type camshaft
angle variator

diameter, on which the twin high lift cams operate, and of a
central tappet of 11 mm diameter, on which the single low
lift cam operates. The low lift tappet directly operates the
valve and contains the zero-lash valve clearance adjuster.
The high lift tappet and the low lift tappet can move up and
down but not rotate independently of each other. At its lower
end the low lift tappet carries an abutment plate for a light
spring ensuring that, in the low lift mode, the external sleeve
returns to its top position when the valves are closed. Both
the low and high lift tappets are in constant contact with their
respective cams.

When the engine operates in the low lift mode, the central
low lift cam acting on the low lift tappet opens the valve
while the two high lift cams operate the high lift tappet which
idles. To change to the high lift mode, the low and high lift
tappets must be locked together. This is achieved by a small
hydraulically operated plunger moving in a cross-drilling
across the two concentric tappets which now operate as
if they were a single solid tappet operated by the high
lift cams.

What happens when?

At idle, the Variocam Plus keeps the intake camshafts at their late base timing, together with low valve lift, resulting in no intake/exhaust valve overlap, flexible operation and low HC (unburnt hydrocarbon) and CO raw emissions*. At part throttle, tappets remain in the low lift mode, up to around 4,000rpm, reducing friction losses when the intake camshaft timing moves towards early opening of the valves to provide valve overlap and achieve a high internal EGR (Exhaust Gas Recirculation) in the interest of lower NOx emissions and lower pumping losses. At higher engine speeds and whenever full throttle is used, the high lift mode is selected, the camshafts progressively return to the late valve opening position to benefit from the late closing of the valves after BDC and exploit the ram effect of the intake charge for a better filling of the cylinders.

Raw emissions are those as exhausted by the engine, upstream of the catalysts.

CAYMAN S MANUAL GEARBOX RATIOS

Gear	Ratio
1st	3.308: 1
2nd	1.950: 1
3rd	1.407: 1
4th	1.133: 1
5th	0.972: 1
6th	0.822: 1
Reverse	3.00: 1

Final drive: 3.875:1

These figures result in an overall final ratio of 3.18:1

in sixth gear and a speed of 24mph at 1,000rpm

TRANSMISSION

Standard transmission is a six-speed manual gearbox in conjunction with a twin-mass flywheel and 240mm diameter clutch. Both units are similar to those of the Boxster S, except for the 1st and 2nd gear ratios, which are slightly taller. Consequently the gearbox ratios are as above.

The optional five-speed Tiptronic transmission is the same as in the Boxster S, except for the shorter 4.161:1 final drive resulting in a speed of 24.9mph in top gear at 1,000rpm and better acceleration.

▼ The rounded roof is a reminder of the 356 coupés

RUNNING GEAR AND BRAKES

The Cayman S running gear is basically identical to that of the Boxster S, except for slightly stiffer springs and anti-roll bars and correspondingly adjusted damping. 18in wheels are standard with 235/40 ZR 18 tyres at the front and 265/40 ZR 18 tyres on the rear. 19in wheels are an option.

The PSM stability management is standard and is tuned as in all other Porsche sports cars to allow a sporting driving style. It can be deactivated, but its function is instantly resumed if the driver brakes hard enough to trigger the ABS on both front wheels. As in the Boxster, the PASM electronic damping and the Sport Chrono Plus are options.

Thanks to its uprated suspension, its ideal weight distribution and its very rigid body structure, the Cayman S is arguably

▲ The drilled and perforated front brake discs and monobloc four-piston aluminium callipers are identical to those of the Boxster S. PCCB brakes are an option

the best handling road-legal Porsche, except possibly for the Carrera GT. This should place it very high up among the world's driver's cars.

As far as straight-line performance is concerned, it logically fits between the Boxster S and the 911 Carrera, as the official factory figures suggest (Tiptronic figures in parentheses).

The fact that the first Cayman model on the market carries the suffix 'S' hints at the probability that at least one slightly less powerful and less luxuriously-equipped model is planned for the future.

▼ All Porsche models are tested extensively under extreme cold and hot conditions

ACCELERATION AND PERFORMANCE FIGURES

		Boxster S	Cayman S	911 Carrera 3.6
0–100km/h (0–62mph)		5.5s (6.3s)	5.4s (6.1s)	5.0s
0–160km/h (0–100mph)		12.3s (13.9s)	11.7s (13.5s)	11.0s
0–200km/h (0–124mph)		20.2s (23.3s)	18.6s (21.6s)	17.5s
0–1,000m		24.9s (25.9s)	24.3s (25.4s)	23.8s
Max speed	(km/h)	268	275	285
	(mph)	166.5	171	177

PRESS COMMENTS

The Cayman S

The first press drives of the Cayman S took place in Tuscany, near Siena. Mark Hales, writing for the *Daily Telegraph*, who also has extensive racing experience, was among the invited journalists. After explaining the major differences between the Cayman S and the Boxster line from which it has been developed, the over-100 per cent increase in its body's torsional stiffness accruing from its closed body and its links with the 997-series 911 Carrera, Mark Hales writes: "On the road, the Cayman S does indeed feel a lot stiffer than the convertible, thanks to its tougher suspension settings, but it still exhibits the same

◀ The Cayman S cockpit differs from the Boxster's only by small details and the upholstery material

kind of delightful front to rear balance – and still without that artificial pointiness that has been added to the front end of some rivals to make them more interesting. It also manages that seductive but controlled float over humps and bumps, dipping and bucking at either one end or the other – something only really well-sorted mid-engined cars can do. Meanwhile it is certainly quick: the 3.4-litre variocam engine pulls and pulls from way down on the dial to

▼ The 19in wheels are an option on the Cayman S

▲ The split aerofoil is unique to the Cayman S, creating increased down force to improve high-speed stability

beyond three figures in third gear, and even if the exhaust note sounds more like a strangled firework the wail that reaches the cabin still sounds exactly like a traditional Porsche flat-six.

"The lesser dynamic details too are nicely sorted: the brakes are firm yet feelsome (the ceramic ones even more so), the steering's variable nature is hardly noticeable (which should be taken as a compliment) and the shift for the six-speed transmission is so easy and accurate, it almost slips into the next ratio for you – and it is almost impossible to shunt the drive line. As a colleague put it, whatever you think of, you get the impression the engineers have been there before you ... Is it a cheaper and slightly more accessible 911 or a dearer and slightly faster Boxster?"

Writing in the *Sunday Times*, Andrew Frankel, another journalist with track experience, writes: "The new car itself is a masterpiece. On paper it doesn't look too exciting: a hard-topped Boxster with a 3.4-litre 295bhp to plug the gap between the 3.2-litre 280bhp Boxster S and the 3.6-litre, 325bhp 911. It is not that quick – its 0–62mph time of 5.4sec would be beaten with ease by a Mercedes-Benz SLK 55 AMG.

None of this matters. All you need to know in performance terms is that the Cayman S is plenty quick enough, but that could never, on its own, make it the exceptional car it is ... Legend has it that cars with their engine behind the driver are inherently more dangerous to drive fast. The Cayman S proves that, with proper design, the legend is nonsense.

"In fact the only really annoying thing about it is that there is pretty little to complain about. It looks a bit awkward from some angles, the standard brakes don't feel as nice as the optional and hideously expensive carbon ceramic discs, the centre console is an ergonomic nightmare; and tall drivers will find it lacking a little legroom. Compared with its mighty talents, it's not much of a list."

At the Cayman S press drives in Italy, Colin Goodwin, writing in *Autocar*, learned that Porsche, anxious that the Cayman S should not cannibalize sales of the 911, had organized market research to find out how many potential 911 customers would opt for a Cayman S instead. The result was only three per cent. "I suspect I know who these people are," Goodwin writes.

▼ A fog light brings some life to the front air intake

▼ The large rear
hatch opens to reveal
a generous 260 litres
of luggage space.
Nets are provided to
secure luggage and a
removable liner (not
shown) covers the
deeper part of the
boot at the rear

"They'll be those who have been intimate with the 911 for many
years and who mourn the passing of the simple 911, when it
was lighter, leaner and less polished. Also they will be people
who loved the philosophy of the 911 Club Sport, RS and the
968 Club Sport: sports cars pared down to their minimum
with a Colin Chapman-like attention for weight saving and an
emotive and direct link to the race track. The Cayman S is the
911-lover's non-911. Though the car is not dramatically lighter
than the 911, barely narrower and just three inches shorter,
it has a very pure and simple feel to it. The hard core
will be praying that Porsche does the proper thing
and builds a Cayman RS or CS. ... At £43,930
the Cayman S neatly fills the gap between

▲ A small hatch in
the rear boot opens
to reveal the oil and
coolant fillers

the Boxster and the 911, and with the cheapest 911 still £16,000 more expensive, there's plenty of scope for further Cayman iterations."

In the 12 October 2005 issue of the Swiss *Automobil Revue*, Hansruedi Ryf, back from the Cayman S test drives in Italy, writes: "The powerful engine pulls strongly with an electrifying sound over almost the entire revolution range. The six-speed manual gearbox convinces with precise shifts requiring minimal force. Its close upper four ratios and the accompanying engine sound animate to much more frequent shifts than the flexible engine really requires. ... Even more impressive than the good performance is the near-perfect handling of the aggressive reptile. In our opinion, the Cayman S reacts noticeably quicker and more accurately than the 911 Carrera to steering inputs and negotiates all sorts of bends and corners with more precision. In addition to the mid-engined configuration, this is surely also a result of the twice-as-high rigidity of the coupé body, compared to the Boxster. ... As expected from a Porsche, the Cayman S impresses with its composed handling

▼ The lower part of the dials is dedicated to digital information including onboard computer data

culminating in very high limits. Driving the car, it is obvious that
Porsche cars are developed on race tracks."

But not everything is perfect and the tester concludes:
"The rear part of the body with a wide C-pillar limits the three-
quarter rear view and the massive head rest of the passenger
seat additionally reduces the visibility through the rear side
window. ... The list of options is long, but those who look for
pure driving pleasure are well cared for with the standard
equipment and can easily dispense with expensive options."

In the November 2005 issue of *Auto*, one of Italy's foremost
car magazines, Alberto Sarasini writes, after the press test
drives in Toscany: "Driving the car is fascinating, even though
the chassis could clearly deal with even more power than the
295bhp of the new flat-six developed from the Boxster S's
3.2-litre, 'embellished' by the 911's cylinder heads, inclusive
of the Variocam Plus valve gear modifying the intake valve
timing and lift. The result is a rather generous torque output at
lower and medium engine speeds, the engine only revealing
its aggressive, racing-like character when 4,000–5,000rpm

▲ **Interior workmanship
of the Cayman S is of a
very high class**

are reached, from where it pushes on nervously to 6,000rpm. Full marks also go to the excellent quick and accurate six-speed close ratio gearbox.

"The handling benefits from a stiffer suspension and a more rigid structure than the roadster, but does not noticeably modify the car's behaviour: the mid-engine configuration results in particularly neutral handling with just-perceptible understeer which progressively increases with rising cornering speeds. There is enough power to create power oversteer (provided the stability control is switched off), but the excellent traction and the particular weight distribution efficiently kill this tendency. Oversteer only happens if provoked. Exceptional as always in a Porsche are the steering and brakes. The first is responsive, direct and accurate and tells you everything about what the front end is doing; the brakes (with the expensive carbon ceramic discs on the test car) offer a peerless efficiency ... Only the initial sensitivity of the pedal requires some getting used to."

In the Belgo-French *Moniteur Automobile*, Xavier Daffe, the magazine's sports car specialist, concludes his report of the

Cayman S test drives as follows: "More than a simple variant of the Boxster, the Cayman S is a new model in its own right. The evolutions from which mainly the engine has benefited notably change its personality, which has become more explosive and hence more sporting. This high-performance two-seater coupé is perfectly suitable for everyday use, being very docile and practical, virtues underlined by 410 litres of luggage space (of which 150 litres are in the front boot and the rest in the back, accessible through a wide rear hatch panel), has the profile of a little, diabolically agile 911, as they were more than twenty years ago, but with the bonus of a behaviour more accessible to ordinary mortals – if only this were also the case of its price!"

One of the first full test reports on the Cayman S was published by the German *Auto Motor und Sport* magazine in its 26 October 2005 issue. The car was burdened with such optional equipment as satellite navigation, leather upholstery, full electric sports seats, 19in wheels, PASM with 'Sport Chrono Plus', xenon headlights and, last but not least, PCCB

▼ The lateral air intakes are ideally placed for efficiency, but the rear quarter panels limit visibility. The very wide doors can be cumbersome in close quarters

▲ Immense grip
is provided by the
optional 35 aspect
ratio on 19in wheels

brakes, increasing the price by some €22,300 and the kerb weight by 75kg to 1,415kg compared to the standard model. For comparison, the Cayman S was accompanied in the road test by a 911 Carrera, the drivers swapping cars as required. Tester Bernd Wieland writes: "After only a few kilometres, it becomes clear that Porsche has put a winner on its optional 19-inch wheels. The compact coupé is extremely agile, turns in keenly and can be placed with millimetric accuracy. It feels more agile than the classic Porsche [911] but also more than the Boxster. Compared to the Cayman, the 911 feels heavier and is more work for the driver. When turning-in, the understeer phase is shorter in the Cayman which 'sucks' itself to the road, reacts quicker and assumes a neutral attitude sooner in the curve. The PSM allows a small amount of oversteer. ... The mid-engined sports car has the quicker reflexes and thus improves on the 911 in the most important of all sports car criteria."

After emphasizing that, thanks to its roof, the torsional rigidity of the Cayman is more than twice that of the Boxster, the tester continues: "This is why the Cayman is less

demanding on the driver and more precise in its behaviour. ...
Thanks to the higher rigidity, the springs, dampers and (front)
anti-roll bar could be made stiffer than in the Boxster. The
result is convincing: the Cayman is in no way too hard and
offers a surprisingly acceptable overall comfort to which the
excellent sports seats also contribute. But everything changes
with a push on the 'Sport' switch in the centre console. The
suspension becomes harsher, the PSM intervenes later and
the response to the electronic throttle pedal becomes sharper,
even if in the normal position the driver would never complain
about throttle response.

"As harmonic as its sound is the rise of the engine's power
output. This is a real sports car engine of which the low inertia
translates into immediate brilliant acceleration ... helped by a
perfect choice of the ratios in the six-speed gearbox of which
the shift quality reminds you that 'paddle shifts' are not an
absolute necessity. ... There will surely be people seeing the
Cayman S as the poor man's 911. Never mind, this is a car
for connoisseurs."

▼ **Tackling this sort of
road with a Cayman S
is pure delight**

Technical & Performance Information

986 SERIES – BOXSTER 2.5 LITRE (1996–1999)

Engine

Type	M96/20
Cylinder bores	Lokasil
Bore x Stroke	85.5 x 72mm
Capacity	2,480cc
Compression ratio	11.0:1
Valve gear	Variocam (Chain)
Valves (four per cylinder)	
Diameter	Intake 33.3mm
	Exhaust 28.1mm
Valve lift	Intake 10mm
	Exhaust 10mm
Timing variation angle	Intake 25°
	Exhaust 0°
Valve opening duration at	
1mm lift (crankshaft degrees)	Intake 210°
	Exhaust 211°
Connecting rods	Steel
Max. power	150kw (204PS) at 6,000rpm
Max. torque	245Nm at 4,500rpm
Max. revolutions	6,600rpm

Gearbox

	Manual	Tiptronic
Type	G86/00	A86/00
Number of ratios	5	5

Transmission

Rear Wheel Drive	Yes
Twin mass flywheel	Yes
Clutch diameter	240mm
Torque converter diameter	254mm
Torque multiplication ratio	1:1.98

Brakes

	Front	Rear
Disc diam. x thickness	298 x 24mm	292 x 20mm
Callipers (number of pistons)	4	4

Dimensions

Length	4,315mm
Width	1,780mm
Height	1,290mm
Wheelbase	2,415mm
Track front	
with 16in wheels	1,465mm
with 17in wheels	1,455mm
Track rear	
with 16in wheels	1,528mm
with 17in wheels	1,508mm
Weight (DIN)	
with manual gearbox	1,250kg
with Tiptronic transmission	1,300kg

986 SERIES – BOXSTER 2.7 LITRE (2000–2002)

Engine

Type	M96/22
Cylinder bores	Lokasil
Bore x Stroke	85.5 x 78mm
Capacity	2,687cc
Compression ratio	11.0:1
Valve gear	Variocam (Chain)
Valves (four per cylinder)	
Diameter	Intake 33.3mm
	Exhaust 28.1mm
Valve lift	Intake 10mm
	Exhaust 10mm
Timing variation angle	Intake 25°
	Exhaust 0°
Valve opening duration at	
1mm lift (crankshaft degrees)	Intake 210°
	Exhaust 211°
Connecting rods	Steel
Max. power	162kw (220PS) at 6,400rpm
Max. torque	260Nm at 4,750rpm
Max. revolutions	7,200rpm

Gearbox

	Manual	Tiptronic
Type	G86/01	A86/01
Number of ratios	5	5

Transmission

Rear Wheel Drive	Yes
Twin mass flywheel	Yes
Clutch diameter	240mm
Torque converter diameter	254mm
Torque multiplication ratio	1:1.98

Brakes

	Front	Rear
Disc diam. x thickness	298 x 24mm	292 x 20mm
Callipers (number of pistons)	4	4

Dimensions

Length	4,315mm
Width	1,780mm
Height	1,290mm
Wheelbase	2,415mm
Track front	
with 16in wheels	1,465mm
with 17in wheels	1,455mm
Track rear	
with 16in wheels	1,528mm
with 17in wheels	1,508mm
Weight (DIN)	
with manual gearbox	1,260kg
with Tiptronic transmission	1,310kg

986 SERIES – BOXSTER S 3.2 LITRE (2000–2002)

Engine

Type	M96/21
Cylinder bores	Lokasil
Bore x Stroke	93 x 78mm
Capacity	3,179cc
Compression ratio	11.0:1
Valve gear	Variocam (Chain)
Valves (four per cylinder)	
Diameter	Intake 37.1mm
	Exhaust 31.5mm
Valve lift	Intake 10mm
	Exhaust 10mm
Timing variation angle	Intake 25°
	Exhaust 0°
Valve opening duration at	
1mm lift (crankshaft degrees)	Intake 226°
	Exhaust 213°
Connecting rods	Steel
Max. power	185kw (252PS) at 6,250rpm
Max. torque	305Nm at 4,500rpm
Max. revolutions	7,200rpm

Gearbox

	Manual	Tiptronic
Type	G86/20	A86/20
Number of ratios	6	5

Transmission

Rear Wheel Drive	Yes
Twin mass flywheel	Yes
Clutch diameter	240mm
Torque converter diameter	254mm
Torque multiplication ratio	1:1.9

Brakes

	Front	Rear
Disc diam. x thickness	318 x 28mm	298 x 24mm
Callipers (number of pistons)	4	4

Dimensions

Length	4,315mm
Width	1,780mm
Height	1,290mm
Wheelbase	2,415mm
Track front	
with 17in wheels	1,455mm
with 18in wheels	1,465mm
Track rear	
with 17in wheels	1,508mm
with 18in wheels	1,504mm
Weight (DIN)	
with manual gearbox	1,295kg
with Tiptronic transmission	1,335kg

986 SERIES – BOXSTER 2.7 LITRE (2003–2004)

Engine

Type	M96/23
Cylinder bores	Lokasil
Bore x Stroke	85.5 x 78mm
Capacity	2,687cc
Compression ratio	11.0:1
Valve gear	Variocam (hydraulic, vanes)
Valves (four per cylinder)	
Diameter	Intake 33.3mm
	Exhaust 28.1mm
Valve lift	Intake 10mm
	Exhaust 10mm
Timing variation angle	Intake 40°
	Exhaust 0°
Valve opening duration at	
1mm lift (crankshaft degrees)	Intake 210°
	Exhaust 211°
Max. power	168kw (228PS) at 6,300rpm
Max. torque	260Nm (192lb ft) at 4,600rpm
Max. revolutions	7,200rpm

Gearbox

	Manual	Tiptronic
Type	G86/01	A86/01
Number of ratios	5	5

Transmission

Rear Wheel Drive	Yes
Twin mass flywheel	Yes
Clutch diameter	240mm
Torque converter diameter	254mm
Torque multiplication ratio	1:1.98

Brakes

	Front	Rear
Disc diam. x thickness	298 x 24mm	292 x 20mm
Callipers (number of pistons)	4	4

Dimensions

Length	4,320mm
Width	1,780mm
Height	1,290mm
with sports suspension	1,280mm
Wheelbase	2,415mm
Track front	
with standard 16in wheels	1,465mm
Track rear	
with standard 16in wheels	1,528mm
Weight (DIN)	
with manual gearbox	1,275kg
with Tiptronic S transmission	1,330kg

986 SERIES – BOXSTER S 3.2 LITRE (2003–2004)

Engine

Type	M96/24
Cylinder bores	Lokasil
Bore x Stroke	93 x 78mm
Capacity	3,179cc
Compression ratio	11.0:1
Valve gear	Variocam (hydraulic, vanes)
Valves (four per cylinder)	
Diameter	Intake 37.1mm
	Exhaust 31.5mm
Valve lift	Intake 10mm
	Exhaust 10mm
Timing variation angle	Intake 40°
	Exhaust 0°
Valve opening duration at	
1mm lift (crankshaft degrees)	Intake 226°
	Exhaust 213°
Max. power	191kw (260PS) at 6,200rpm
Max. torque	310Nm (228.5lb ft) at 4,600rpm
Max. revolutions	7,200rpm

Gearbox

Gearbox	Manual	Tiptronic
Type	G86/20	A86/20
Number of ratios	6	5

Transmission

Rear Wheel Drive	Yes
Twin mass flywheel	Yes
Clutch diameter	240mm
Torque converter diameter	254mm
Torque multiplication ratio	1:1.9

Brakes

Brakes	Front	Rear
Disc diam. x thickness	318 x 28mm	299 x 24mm
Callipers (number of pistons)	4	4

Dimensions

Length	4,320mm
Width	1,780mm
Height	1,290mm
with sports suspension	1,280mm
Wheelbase	2,415mm
Track front	
with standard 17in wheels	1,455mm
Track rear	
with standard 17in wheels	1,514mm
Weight (DIN)	
with manual gearbox	1,320kg
with Tiptronic S transmission	1,360kg

987 SERIES – BOXSTER 2.7 LITRE (2005–)

Engine

Type	M96/25
Cylinder bores	Lokasil
Bore x Stroke	85.5 x 78mm
Capacity	2,687cc
Compression ratio	11.0:1
Valve gear	Variocam (hydraulic, vanes)
Valves (four per cylinder)	
Diameter	Intake 33.3mm
	Exhaust 28.1mm
Valve lift	Intake 10mm
	Exhaust 10mm
Timing variation angle	Intake 40°
	Exhaust 0°
Valve opening duration at	
1mm lift (crankshaft degrees)	Intake 210°
	Exhaust 211°
Max. power	176kw (240PS) at 6,400rpm
Max. torque	270Nm (199lb ft)
	at 4,700–6,000rpm
Max. revolutions	7,200rpm

Gearbox

	Manual	Tiptronic
Type	G87/00	A87/01
Number of ratios	5 (6 opt)	5

Transmission

Rear Wheel Drive	Yes
Twin mass flywheel	Yes
Clutch diameter	240mm
Torque converter diameter	254mm
Torque multiplication ratio	1:1.98

Brakes

	Front	Rear
Disc diam. x thickness	298 x 24mm	299 x 20mm
Callipers (number of pistons)	4	4

Dimensions

Length	4,329mm
Width	1,801mm
Height	1,295mm
with PASM	1,285mm
Wheelbase	2,415mm
Track front	
with standard 17in wheels	1,490mm
Track rear	
with standard 17in wheels	1,534mm
Weight (DIN)	
with manual gearbox	1,295kg
with Tiptronic S transmission	1,355kg

987 SERIES – BOXSTER S 3.2 LITRE (2005–)

Engine

Type	M96/26
Cylinder bores	Lokasil
Bore x Stroke	93 x 78mm
Capacity	3,179cc
Compression ratio	11.0:1
Valve gear	Variocam (hydraulic, vanes)
Valves (four per cylinder)	
Diameter	Intake 37.1mm
	Exhaust 31.5mm
Valve lift	Intake 10mm
	Exhaust 10mm
Timing variation angle	Intake 40°
	Exhaust 0°
Valve opening duration at	
1mm lift (crankshaft degrees)	Intake 226°
	Exhaust 213°
Max. power	206kw (280PS) at 6,400rpm
Max. torque	320Nm (236lb ft)
	at 4,700–6,000rpm
Max. revolutions	7,200rpm

Gearbox

	Manual	Tiptronic
Type	G87/20	A87/20
Number of ratios	6	5

Transmission

Rear Wheel Drive	Yes
Twin mass flywheel	Yes
Clutch diameter	240mm
Torque converter diameter	254mm
Torque multiplication ratio	1:1.9

Brakes

	Front	Rear
Disc diam. x thickness	318 x 28mm	299 x 24mm
Callipers (number of pistons)	4	4

Dimensions

Length	4,329mm
Width	1,801mm
Height	1,295mm
with PASM	1,285mm
Wheelbase	2,415mm
Track front	
with standard 18in wheels	1,486mm
Track rear	
with standard 18in wheels	1,528mm
Weight (DIN)	
with manual gearbox	1,345kg
with Tiptronic S transmission	1,385kg

CAYMAN S 3.4 LITRE (2005–)

Engine

Type	M97/21
Cylinder bores	Lokasil
Bore x Stroke	96 x 78mm
Capacity	3,386cc
Compression ratio	11.1:1
Valve gear	Variocam Plus
Valves (four per cylinder)	
Diameter	Intake 40.2mm
	Exhaust 34.5mm
Valve lift	Intake 11mm
	Exhaust 11mm
Timing variation angle	Intake 40°
	Exhaust 0°
Valve opening duration at	
1mm lift (crankshaft degrees)	Intake 229°/122°
	Exhaust 225.5°
Max. power	217kw (295PS) at 6,250rpm
Max. torque	340Nm (251lb ft)
	at 4,400–6,000rpm
Max. revolutions	7,300rpm

Gearbox

	Manual	Tiptronic
Type	G87/21	A87/21
Number of ratios	6	5

Transmission

Rear Wheel Drive	Yes
Twin mass flywheel	Yes
Clutch diameter	240mm
Torque converter diameter	254mm
Torque multiplication ratio	1:1.9

Brakes

	Front	Rear
Disc diam. x thickness	318 x 28mm	299 x 24mm
Callipers (number of pistons)	4	4

Dimensions

Length	4,341mm
Width	1,801mm
Height	1,305mm
with PASM	1,295mm
Wheelbase	2,415mm
Track front	
with standard 18in wheels	1,486mm
Track rear	
with standard 18in wheels	1,528mm
Weight (DIN)	
with manual gearbox	1,340kg
with Tiptronic S transmission	1,395kg

PERFORMANCE FIGURES

Porsche Data (DIN weight + ½ payload)	Boxster 2.5 (1996–1999) 204PS(DIN)	Boxster 2.7 (2000–2002) 220PS(DIN)	Boxster S 3.2 (2000–2002) 252PS(DIN)
0–100km/h (s)	6.6 (Tip 7.6)	6.6 (Tip 7.4)	5.9 (Tip 6.5)
0–160km/h (s)	16.5 (Tip 18.9)	15.9 (Tip 17.4)	13.8 (Tip 15.1)
0–200km/h (s)	–	–	–
Standing km (s)	27.4 (Tip 28.0)	26.8 (Tip 27.8)	25.6 (Tip 26.5)
V-max (km/h)	240 (Tip 235)	250 (Tip 245)	260 (Tip 255)

Auto Motor und Sport (Manual Gearbox)	Boxster 2.5 (1996–1999) 204PS(DIN)	Boxster 2.7 (2000–2002) 220PS(DIN)	Boxster S 3.2 (2000–2002) 252PS(DIN)
0–100km/h (s)	7.1	6.8	6.1
0–160km/h (s)	17.8	15.8	14.2
0–200km/h (s)	33.0	27.2	24.2
Standing km (s)	27.5	26.9	26.0
V-max (km/h)	240 (149mph)	250 (155mph)	260 (161.5mph)

Automobil Revue (Manual Gearbox)	Boxster 2.5 (1996–1999) 204PS(DIN)	Boxster 2.7 (2000–2002) 220PS(DIN)	Boxster S 3.2 (2000–2002) 252PS(DIN)
0–100km/h (s)	6.8	–	5.7
0–160km/h (s)	16.9	–	13.3
0–200km/h (s)	–	–	–
Standing km (s)	26.9	–	25.5
V-max (km/h)	241 (150mph)	–	260 (161.5mph)

Autocar (Manual Gearbox)	Boxster 2.5 (1996–1999) 204PS(DIN)	Boxster 2.7 (2000–2002) 220PS(DIN)	Boxster S 3.2 (2000–2002) 252PS(DIN)
0–60mph (s)	6.5 (Tip 7.3)	6.4	6.0
0–100mph (s)	16.9 (Tip 19.1)	15.5	14.2
V-max (mph)	139 (Tip 136)	149	161

Manufacturer's Data and Road Test Data obtained by:
Auto Motor und Sport (Germany), *Autocar* (Great Britain) and *Automobil Revue* (Switzerland)

PERFORMANCE FIGURES

Boxster 2.7 (2003–2004) 228PS(DIN)	Boxster S 3.2 (2003–2004) 260PS(DIN)	Boxster 2.7 (2005–) 240PS(DIN)	Boxster S 3.2 (2005–) 280PS(DIN)	Cayman S 3.4 (2005–) 295PS(DIN)
6.4 (Tip 7.3)	5.7 (Tip 6.4)	6.2 (Tip 7.1)	5.5 (Tip 6.3)	5.4 (Tip 6.1)
15.0 (Tip 17.2)	13.2 (Tip 14.9)	14.5 (Tip 16.4)	12.3 (Tip 13.9)	11.7 (Tip 13.5)
–	–	24.6 (Tip 27.2)	20.2 (Tip 23.3)	18.6 (Tip 21.6)
26.5 (Tip 27.6)	25.3 (Tip 26.3)	26.2 (Tip 27.2)	24.9 (Tip 25.9)	24.3 (Tip 25.4)
253 (Tip 248)	264 (Tip 258)	256 (Tip 250)	268 (Tip 260)	275 (Tip 267)

Boxster 2.7 (2003–2004) 228PS(DIN)	Boxster S 3.2 (2003–2004) 260PS(DIN)	Boxster 2.7 (2005–) 240PS(DIN)	Boxster S 3.2 (2005–) 280PS(DIN)	Cayman S 3.4 (2005–) 295PS(DIN)
6.2	5.7	–	5.4	5.5
14.4	13.6	–	12.4	12.0
–	22.1	–	20.2	19.2
26.0	25.4	–	–	–
253 (157mph)	264 (164mph)	–	268 (168mph)	275 (171mph)

Boxster 2.7 (2003–2004) 228PS(DIN)	Boxster S 3.2 (2003–2004) 260PS(DIN)	Boxster 2.7 (2005–) 240PS(DIN)	Boxster S 3.2 (2005–) 280PS(DIN)	Cayman S 3.4 (2005–) 295PS(DIN)
–	5.7	–	–	–
–	13.6	–	–	–
–	–	–	–	–
–	25.6	–	–	–
–	264 (164mph)	–	–	–

Boxster 2.7 (2003–2004) 228PS(DIN)	Boxster S 3.2 (2003–2004) 260PS(DIN)	Boxster 2.7 (2005–) 240PS(DIN)	Boxster S 3.2 (2005–) 280PS(DIN)	Cayman S 3.4 (2005–) 295PS(DIN)
6.3	–	6.1	–	5.4
15.2	–	15.1	–	–
155	–	157	–	–

Manufacturer's Data and Road Test Data obtained by:
Auto Motor und Sport (Germany), *Autocar* (Great Britain) and *Automobil Revue* (Switzerland)

Index